BACKSTAGE PASS

MUM
1945 – 2021

You will always be with us,
in our hearts,
memories and
lives forever.
Love you.

אין עוד כאב

BACKSTAGE PASS

A business book that's *far* from conventional

50% Rock and Roll

50% Business

100% True

HARVEY LEE

harvey-lee.com
DEFINITION BOOKS
London | UK
Definition Books is an imprint of Definition Music Limited

DEFINITION BOOKS●

First published 2024
Edition 001

Copyright © Harvey Lee, 2022
All photographs © Harvey Lee, 1973 – 2023, except where indicated
My sincere thanks to Tony Roffe and Mike Stone

The moral right of the author has been asserted

Set in Garamond Premier Pro

Printed by Lightning Source

A CIP catalogue record for this book is available from the British Library

Hardcover ISBN: 978-1-916580-00-8
Trade Paperback ISBN: 978-1-916580-01-5
eBook ISBN: 978-1-916580-02-2
Audiobook ISBN: 978-1-916580-05-3

CONTENTS

AUTHOR'S NOTE

This book is the first part of my story. It's mine, and mine alone – others may have different recollections. I have not set out to embarrass or offend anyone, and I sincerely hope I have not done so. I have changed some minor details out of respect for the privacy of some individuals.

H.L. – London, 2022

CHAPTER 1

BAT OUT OF HELL

Mr. Clough, my sadistic music teacher, held me by my wrist and gave me one strong swipe on my fingertips per word.

"I (swipe) said (swipe) no (swipe) talking (swipe) in (swipe) class (swipe). Okay?" He raised the slipper higher, and it came crashing down on the full palm of my hand.

Other times it was my arse. This was the worst and one feared amongst the class. He used the cane and the sadistic streak was evident. He was relishing, revelling in the act itself.

How did we know? You'd be told to bend over the large, black grand piano in the corner of the music room and lift the back of your school blazer (sports coat). You knew what was coming, and that's why most of the class clenched their fists and buttocks and looked at the floor.

He'd hold up the cane above and behind his head, start a long-crazed run up from the other side of the room akin to a long jumper, and whack! He'd hit you so hard that both of *his* feet would lift off the ground. Then, almost to emphasise his seemingly proud sadism, he'd put on some classical music on the record player, sit back and listen in silence. All he needed was a cigarette.

We'd all have to sit there in silence until he collected his composure and continued with the class, ignoring whatever carnage he'd caused on his victim. Smoking in school was banned. But beating the crap out of the pupils was not.

I did love music, just not the kind Mr. Clough approved of. I had been days away from my twelfth birthday when AC/DC released their seminal album *Back in Black* on 25th July 1980. No one knew then that it would be the best-selling rock album of all time and the second best-selling album of all time, only eclipsed by Michael Jackson's *Thriller*. No one had any idea. Not even the band themselves.

Looking back, it seems such an abstract concept that a single album could have shaped my life so much. An album of such importance to the band after tragically losing their singer Bon Scott, just when they had broken through internationally in 1979. It carried so much emotion from deep inside the band that you couldn't ignore the statement they made with this record. They had a point to prove, and it's hallmarked on every track on this landmark album.

A couple of years later, I saw AC/DC live in concert on October 3rd 1982, at the Apollo Theatre, Manchester. It left me breathless (and slightly hard of hearing!), and for the first time, I'd felt what motivation felt like – not being told what to do but knowing what I wanted to do.

I'd wanted to be in a band and feel that raw electric power in my own hands. Slight problem, though, I couldn't play an instrument and had no proven talent. So, that's why I'd signed up for music class at school and put myself at the mercy of Mr. Clough.

I did put the effort in, stayed after class, tried instruments (including the triangle!), made a dismal racket, and gave this avenue up. There's only so far trombones and kettle drums will get you if you want to be in a rock band.

The one good thing about music class was Jimmy Taylor. He was cool. He had long hair, played the drums, and looked like Tommy Lee from Motley Crüe, the new hot band on the scene. We chatted about AC/DC and Twisted Sister, another band we nerded over, and he invited me to his house one day.

Jimmy only lived a 15-minute walk away, and I made two monumental discoveries on my first visit. He played in a band and his parents had converted half their garage into a rehearsal room. His bandmates were Paul Yung, a lanky guitar player who looked like he belonged in an LA big-hair metal band, and Loz on bass, who, to be frank, was more conventional. A bit like me. They invited me to sit in and played through semi-recognisable versions of Twisted Sister songs from the *Under The Blade* (1982) album. Something was missing... singing! No one was singing, even though there was a microphone there. I saw my chance and said, "Hey, I can hold a tune!"

(Really? Could I hold a tune? In reality, I'd sang in the school choir when I was much younger, but that's about it. Fake it till you make it!)

One quick audition of 'Shoot'em Down' by Twisted Sister and I was in! Admittedly, with modest talent and limited ability, we never played to anyone else or left the garage. But it didn't matter to me. I'd found a way to make it happen and that was good enough for now.

And it was around this time, at 14, that my formal education started to go astray. Rock music, life around rock music, and smoking cigarettes were way more interesting than school.

As my apathy for school grew, the less the school seemed to care. It appears that pea-shooting my math teacher in class, looking up the skirt of my hot art teacher, or throwing a pencil eraser across an exam hall only to lodge in the ample cleavage of Mrs. Turner did my cause no good at all!

I'd spend my days on the playing fields, smoking with a

newfound friend called Andy. We'd talk rubbish. As far as the school records were concerned, I was at school. I'd turn up morning and afternoon, be there for registration, and then brazenly walk out. It's still a mystery to me that no one seemingly cared, or even tried to help. It felt like I was just written off, and I accepted it.

But the underlying reason wasn't a mystery to me. I was being bullied, a victim of violent antisemitism in a school of indifference, and hundreds of Christian kids. It started with being excluded, name-called, and then getting badly beaten up in the playground. Regularly.

The bullying only stopped after I eventually snapped and fought one kid back on the playing field. Surrounded by a circle of 30 kids chanting "fight, fight, fight," egging us on as they all relentlessly spat on us to tease us out of our standoff. I dodged the first punch and then took the fight to him; he came off worse.

Even though I had my 'Rocky' moment, I didn't feel victorious, despite the cheers of the baying crowd. I was done. I was done with school, done with not having any support from those who were *supposed* to be providing safeguarding; I figured no one cared, and it shaped my irreverent attitude at the time. Rather than make a complaint, the illogical shame of being a victim of bullying led me down a different path.

I had bunked off school for two years, and no one noticed.

My poor parents had no idea this was happening until I left school. My school leaving report was a damning indictment of my lack of achievement.

"Harvey hasn't taken advantage of the opportunities available to him," it said. C, D, and E are hardly grades you or your parents would be proud of. I wasn't ashamed because I didn't even care.

The scale of my indifference led me to light up a cigarette on the school campus on my last day as I went around to collect signatures from my teachers to acknowledge that I'd handed all the relevant books back before I left. The Deputy Headmaster Mr. Peters caught me, grabbed me by the collar, and for the first time, contacted my parents.

He threatened to withhold my leaving report. Great, I thought, it's terrible anyway, better we don't read it! Typical of my Dad, he got on the phone and sorted it out, and when the school leaving report arrived, nothing good happened from there on in.

I'd been antagonising my parents off and on for a couple of years and had generally been a terrible teen. They might've hoped that my school report would've been reasonable as I wasn't stupid, and they saw me leave each morning to go there. Only you know I didn't, and if they're reading this, so do my parents!

And so, I left school aged 15, parents steaming over a school leaving report that lacked any silver lining at all. The thing I latched onto was a comment from the Headmaster, which has stuck with me all this time.

"Harvey has not reaped the opportunities available to him... but he does get on well with others, particularly those who have a real interest in rock music."

I didn't know at the time that this was to be the basis of my future career path.

As an unqualified school leaver in 1980s Britain, I had limited options regarding where to look for work. I could write speculative letters to big organisations, go to The Job Centre or reply to classified adverts in the local newspaper. I did it all. I also learnt quite quickly that my options were limited to a mixture of what I didn't want to do, couldn't do, or wasn't qualified to do. The biggest issue was that I didn't know what I *did* want to do.

The Job Centre was a grim place. A place where the lost went to see what they could find. In this place, £2 per hour seemed like a lottery win. Still, when a pack of cigarettes cost about £1.35, your 'winnings' would slip through your fingers (or into your lungs) very quickly, and 'bin man', 'driver', or 'waitress' were occupations that were top of the aspirational ladder. It was a place of manual or administerial work only. I learned what I didn't want to do here, but given my somewhat self-made circumstances, I kept visiting as the workforce authorities made school leavers attend.

Writing letters for advertised jobs was another new experience and a grounding one. All the jobs that looked good to me required a certain level of qualifications, and to a large degree, this has not changed over the years. Still, I'll go into this in more detail later in the book, as there's a tipping point where the requirements become less critical.

I got the help of my Dad on this one. My Dad was, as far as I was concerned, an expert letter writer. After all, he'd had enough practice. Every time there was something to complain about, the pen and paper came out, as if they were sword and shield, preparing for battle. And off went a well-crafted complaint that put the unassuming recipient on life support. He'd put them to the sword. The results were precise... usually, a full refund or voucher for something with an apology would turn up in the post by return. Occasionally, the response would be a phone call from a representative falling over themselves to apologise. Dad had an internal 'grovel meter'; the more they grovelled, the more satisfaction he felt.

If the compensation value outweighed the original purchase value and the grovel meter scored high enough, then out came the Mick Jagger impersonation! Clapping hands and singing, yes, "I can't get no... satisfaction!" Highly embarrassing to witness as a teenager.

But I did learn about the power of words.

Mick Jagger impersonations aside, we sat at the kitchen table, and he gave me advice on how to write an excellent basic letter. English was one of the subjects at school that I was good at, and there were two good reasons for this:

1. It was something creative; I found I could use words creatively to communicate how I felt or thought, and
2. My teacher was excellent.

How do I qualify this? Yes, he knew his stuff, but so did all the other teachers. The difference here was his relationship with the pupils. He was much younger than most of the other teachers. He had empathy and awareness, he visibly cared, and with me, he saw someone who was somewhat lost in the system (you could claim failed by the system) but, critically, had the ability.

He knew where my interests lay and where he could, he would base work around my interests and get the best out of me. It was no accident that English was my best subject at school and the *only* subject where I got a decent exam pass. I'm grateful to him for taking the time to give me some focus and realising that one-size-does-not always fit all.

So, back to the kitchen table. Rules around paragraphs, addressing people, signing off, the rules, the exception to the rules, structure, we went through it all. And at the end of it, I became quite a good letter writer.

But it didn't achieve its objective. Straight-A rejections, citing lack of experience and qualifications. It was disheartening, but hardly surprising.

I lowered my sights and started to apply for jobs in the local papers. There were plenty listed; however, given the nature of these listings, it was a game of lucky dip. You had no idea who the job was with or that, given the 'help wanted' nature of the ads, there was limited space to put many details, so you applied somewhat blindfolded.

I applied for a few and quickly learnt that you can't take these at face value. I got a callback or letter from one application with an 'interview' at a prime location in the city centre. Suit on, I thought, this is it! It wasn't. I was in a room with 50 other 'suits', and they were selling to us! The 'company' was operating a dodgy sales scheme that paid commission only. I think I was asked for money as a deposit for something too. So, I went through a few of these and learnt to sniff them out before I bothered putting a suit on.

But I did get one bite from a company I'd heard of. Would this be my first job?

KEY LESSONS IN LIFE AND BUSINESS

MOTIVATION IS SO IMPORTANT

I had yet to learn what motivated me academically while at school, but I discovered rock music and AC/DC certainly inspired me emotionally. It made me driven.

Scott Galloway at NYU Stern School of Business says in his book 'The Four', "Don't follow your passion; follow your talent. Determine what you are good at (early) and commit to becoming great at it. You don't have to love it; don't hate it. If practice takes you from good to great, the recognition and compensation you will command will make you start to love it.

"And, ultimately, you will be able to shape your career and your speciality to focus on the aspects you enjoy the most. And if not – make good money and then go follow your passion."

Knowing what you *don't* want to do can be as valuable as knowing what you want to do.

Rock music was what I was passionate about, but I wasn't good at it. And I knew it. I knew I wasn't a very good guitar player. And I wasn't a great singer. But 15-year-old me wanted to be a rock star.

As I've learned more about myself over the years, I've realised that when I'm motivated about something, I'm *highly* motivated. **I'll do it better than anyone else.** I'm not about breadth; I'm about depth, but with quite a narrow focus. This could be why I've ended up in product marketing.

ALWAYS HAVE A POINT TO PROVE

I always have a point to prove; maybe it's impostor syndrome. My teachers used to talk down to me and ridicule me, and I left school feeling demoralised. I could either let them beat me and accept it and get a dull, low-grade job forever, or I could come out fighting. I didn't know how to do it, as I was only 15, but I learnt.

Even today, in every job I've had in big companies, **I've always had a point to prove.** I've got a remit in every position (including currently as VP at the Product Marketing Alliance). And I'll consider myself unsuccessful if I don't prove to myself that I can do it. I am a success *despite* my education.

LEARN THE POWER OF WORDS

In a world of emoticons, the art of writing is a dwindling skill but still remains a key communication tool and an asset if you can do it well.

When I was out of school and looking for work, my dad taught me the power of words and the importance of being a good communicator. I still put what he taught me into practice today, and I consider that this book would not have been possible without my dad's guidance when I was a teen.

From these lessons with my dad, I realised I had to be realistic. Yeah, I wanted to be a rock star, but my first job would be a tedious, standard, entry-level job.

Learning to deal with rejection is a crucial part of life, as is having the persistence and tenacity required to overcome that rejection and overcome challenges. You have to try, try and try again.

I've been made redundant twice in the past five years, and my friends and family always say the same thing, "Harvey, you always land on your feet." I don't think this happens by accident or because of luck, but **maybe I land on my feet because I work hard at it.**

CHAPTER 2

DON'T DREAM IT'S OVER

"**W**ill you put that cigarette down! Harvey, if I have to tell you one more time... I'll lose the plot. You CAN NOT smoke in the shop," said my typically mild-mannered manager.

I apologised, but as soon as he went on his break, I lit another one and moved an ashtray under the till counter.

Four weeks into my first job at Young's Formalwear for Men, I was failing. Working was a somewhat surreal experience. The main problem I had was that I didn't adjust or think to adjust; I would later learn (the hard way) that this would be a big mistake.

Young's was a menswear hire shop next door to Pronuptia de Paris, which was in the business of selling the wedding dress dream to future brides. Or at least renting it. And it was where careers went to die.

It was the kind of place where you would hire a wedding suit. Or top hat and tails if you're attending a key event for the upper-crust horse racing calendar. My job was to serve customers in the shop, manage the order book and inventory, and steam press in the back room.

But I spent most of my time smoking and flirting with

Stephanie in the wedding dress shop next door, whilst dreaming about how I would spend my wages (£41 a week).

(Moving from parental donations of pocket money to my own money was a liberating experience. I spent my first wage packet on the latest AC/DC album. £2.50 from HMV. And it felt good. *Really* good.)

Whenever I had to measure someone's inside leg, I had to make sure that I composed myself if I went a bit too high and brushed their crown jewels!

There would be knowing eye contact with the customer. And a very awkward silence, followed by a convenient feeling of denial that it ever happened.

Things ticked over until Royal Ascot Week. Ascot is one of the big races in the English horse racing calendar and is renowned for people dressing up as it's a 'Royal' event. The Queen used to attend. And so, formal dress hire stores up and down the country would make a booming trade, and we were no different. Our entire inventory was booked out a month in advance. There was absolutely nothing left.

One Monday morning, an arrogant man barged into the shop, and I could tell I was about to have my first brush with a problematic customer.

I measured him up, knowing it was likely we could not help him. He told me he needed it that day as he was going to Ascot. I said I'd try to help, but it was unlikely that we could. We went through every line we stocked, and nothing was available in his size.

Despite this, he started to get agitated and told me we must have some backup stock somewhere; he was pushing it, knowing his options were slim given that race day was so close. We honestly had nothing. Our other shops had nothing. He pushed some more. Where was the manager? Good question; where was the manager? Regardless, it was just him and me, and he pushed my buttons once too many times.

"Listen," I told him. "I've tried to help you; there's nothing more I can do. I can't magic a morning suit and top hat up for you, as you're so late coming to us. So, why don't you just fuck off to Moss Bros. [competitor] and see what they've got for you?"

That got him out of the shop! I lit a cigarette and completely forgot about the incident; such was my ambivalence. About a week later, the store manager called me to the back of the shop. The customer had made an official complaint to the area manager. And as the saying went on *The Apprentice* TV show: "You're Fired," complete with the finger point.

I collected my brown envelope containing what was owed to me and left. My attitude and naivety led me to this outcome.

I wasn't in the slightest bit bothered about being fired as I'd already secured a new job at Marks & Spencer, so I had been about to resign anyway.

Marks & Spencer (M&S) is a middle-class shopping institution in Britain. It's known for its quality and service. It was *the* bastion of the main shopping streets in the UK. And my Dad was a career branch manager there. The topic of the son following the father's footsteps came up in the house more than once, and I had no objection to it.

Long story (that I can't remember!) short, my Dad helped me get on a training scheme at M&S in Stockport, a market town just a few miles from its big brother, Manchester.

Similar to an apprenticeship, the Youth Training Scheme (YTS) was an official Government program that involved employers taking school leavers on at 16 and giving them 12 months of work experience and vocational training. You'd work full-time for a 'training allowance' of £26.25 per week. Reputable employers would look to the YTS in-take as making oven-ready candidates for bona fide full-time roles for when the training scheme finished. And usually, those on the schemes with the better employers wanted to be taken on. I was certainly open to it but not married to the idea. I *still* had no idea what I wanted to do.

So, I did the interviews, made nice, and despite getting less money, I saw the value in working for a genuine bona fide employer and getting reputable vocational training. It may've been the factor that my Dad was well-known in the company, but somehow, I got into the scheme. Not only that. The scheme didn't officially start for six weeks, and I was lucky to be offered a part-time, temporary contract for six weeks that ran straight into the training scheme.

Those six weeks were great. I felt the power and rigour of what it was like to work for a big organisation, and despite my previous attitude, I felt myself fitting in – getting on with co-workers. I was respecting the customers, company processes and learning *why* we did things in particular ways and how it synced with the company's values.

I worked in the menswear department for that pre-training scheme contract. Maybe because I came from a menswear back-ground (typecast after just a few weeks at Young's). Regardless, I welcomed the familiarity.

I also welcomed the money! I got paid by the hour for the first time, and the rate was like nothing I'd ever seen. I would make in the morning what I got as weekly pocket money just two months before. And I was still only 15.

And then, one day, there was a drama that has stayed with me to this day. Menswear was next to ladies' lingerie, and let's just say that M&S were quite well known for their knickers.

Before you put 2+2 together and come up with 5, I often needed to venture into knicker-land as customer services, the place you'd return items, was located right next to it. The store layout was designed by a man with a sense of humour. Or a pervert. Either way, I had a business need to be at customer services most days… baggin' an eyeful of what bra-bados had to offer. Hard life. Ahem… er… OK, back to the story.

The day before my YTS placement started, I was walking past a display of racy clothing (again!), and I saw a 'rustling' of the clothes display. The kind of 'rustling' you'd see in a nature program that was secretly filming a pack of secretive animals. Only this mysterious animal was hiding from me. And just like a well-seasoned nature reporter, I had to go in and investigate.

And my, what a find! Was it a female of the species lost in choice? No. Was it an employee fighting with an arm full of inventory? No. It was Mr Heldon, one of my old teachers!

If you've ever heard of the phrase 'like a rabbit in the head-lights of a car', this was more like a rabbit in the headlights of a fleet of trucks!

"Hello, Mr Heldon. Can I help you?" I said with a poker face.

I could hear his heart beating like it was amplified through the store's PA system. An armful of 'this-is-not-really-for-your-wife-is-it-dear,' defied gravity and hit the floor quicker than a groupie's knickers at a rock concert.

And so, the YTS started, as did the pay cut. I felt like I was back on pocket money again. I did embrace the opportunity because I could see a real job at the end of the scheme that I could settle in. Dad would be proud. Or at least *not embarrassed.*

I give M&S credit here; they took their training seriously. We weren't just cheap labour; they treated us as the next potential intake, with respect; it was in their interests too. There were three of us, me and two new girls. We set about our basic train-ing together, and then we were allocated to departments. I was assigned to fresh food – a more dynamic department than the relative sleepiness of menswear.

In reality, it meant keeping the shelves stocked with fruit and vegetables – high turnover inventory. When needed, we had to go upstairs to the warehouse, into the walk-in fridges and grab trolleys of stock, and take them to the shop floor. I worked the cash registers (pre-bar code!) and helped little old ladies find jars of pickled onions. It was OK, but there was a standout memory... what I refer to as the Christmas Eve Turkey Run.

In the weeks before Christmas, customers would place an advanced order for a fresh turkey, and on Christmas Eve, they would be available for anyone with an advanced order. M&S had special opening hours on Christmas Eve. Doors opened at 8am. At 7.45am, there was a queue of 800 housewives outside.

There wasn't enough space on the shelves for all these custom-ordered turkeys. So, we were told to leave them in the warehouse trolleys and wheel them onto the shop floor. Our job was to ensure the birds got into the hands of people who'd ordered and pre-paid for them.

We were looking at the store clock as the long hand struck 8 o'clock. The warehouse guys (as they usually did) jangled their keys and opened the doors on time. Usually, you'd know the doors were open because one or two people would waltz in slowly as if their morning coffee was yet to kick in. Or a piece of litter would waft in off the street and brush over your feet.

In this specific case, there was anticipation in the air, given that hundreds of anxious middle-class housewives were about to have a personality transplant in front of my very eyes. Albeit temporarily. I had been forewarned, but nothing prepared me for it. *Nothing.*

Jangle, jangle went the keys. The doors weren't opened; they were BLASTED open by the sheer force of nature of rabid, middle-aged, turkey-demanding housewives. I heard it before I saw it, given that the food department was in the basement. The rumble. The rumble of 800 pairs of comfortable shoes descending the stairs like a tidal wave, accompanied by the chatter of Gladiatorial elbow jostling for a position to get nearest to the front.

Then I saw it. Like a tsunami of moving brown wool coats and hats, they engulfed the fresh food department. Do you think I had a chance to make sure the right turkey went to the right customer? I was completely surrounded and pinned to the warehouse trolleys by the sheer force of the Turkey Run. The physics of gravity were rewritten for a few minutes as my feet seemed not to touch the ground until it was all over.

Ten minutes later, there wasn't a single turkey left. The metal trolleys were damaged, and my uniform was ripped to shreds. Like Justin Bieber's clothes would be if he just walked down the street during the school holidays.

My year went by quickly, with most of my time spent in the food department, but when my hair began to get a bit longer (past the top of my shirt collar), I got posted to the warehouse, out of sight of customers. The dress code was stringent, and tolerance in the 1980s was not like in the 2020s. I liked the warehouse; the guys there were up for a laugh, many of them ex-forces. I spent much time in the giant fridges and freezers, wheeling stuff around.

It was here, in the warehouse, I had my first experience with 'technology'. I heard it first; I remember four burly warehouse men struggling to lift this giant sideways wardrobe. 'Wardrobe' might be a slight exaggeration. But it was *huge.* It was... one of the new fax machines we'd heard people talk about.

We all stood around as one of the experienced supervisors gave us a demo. Keypad, bang in the number to send it through, wait for 'that' sound, and then, the magic moment. We all stood in awe as we watched a single piece of paper 'disappear' into the machine but then come out of the other end. We thought we'd sent it to ourselves! The 'Super' repeated this process over and over, thinking the paper was supposed to disappear.

As if our fax machine was shredding it and stuffing it down the phone line, and the receiving fax machine was glueing it back together! That's how it worked in our minds.

The concept of something going down a telephone line that was not a voice was an alien concept. We weren't sure what we saw. Until someone from the office upstairs brought a copy of what she'd received, it was our fax! Many copies of our fax!

It was some sort of voodoo magic. How little we knew then, eh? Back to work.

Before I knew it, the year was up, and the reckoning was about to happen. There were two full-time jobs available to the trainees on the YTS. There were three trainees in the scheme. I'm no Einstein, but even I knew three into two meant someone was leaving employment.

It was me.

The reason? My appearance was 'unkempt' as my hair had touched my shirt collar, and the girls were perfect and wholesome in that regard. It sounded like bullshit to my inner rebel, as they didn't have a better reason, but one thing became true during my time at M&S.

I had started performing in a band, playing in public. I'd taken playing in a garage to the next level and was loving it. Being *in* Rock and Roll meant more to me.

M&S did give me another temporary contract for a few months over another Christmas period, so I had another Turkey Run to endure, but this time, it was on full pay. And so it came to pass; Christmas came and went. And along with the turkeys, I'd had my chips.

Of course, I'd known for a while that I'd be leaving M&S, and I found it difficult (at 16 years old and a bit) to think about what was next. I still had no clue, professionally speaking. My Mum knew quite a few people in the local community. She learnt that someone we knew of was moving their business very near to where we lived, and he was on the lookout for some help.

He was a butcher. The Job Centre started looking more and more attractive. But I needed a gig, the type with money and no guitars.

The positive was it was only a 10-minute walk from our house. The downside? Everything else. Mr Vassell was a well-known local butcher, and all my mum's friends went to him, who tended to be my friends' parents. I had to wear a white coat with a hair net. The ridicule and embarrassment were complete.

I hated it. I was so bored that I turned clock-watching into a professional sport. The job was just tending the shop front, serving steaks and deli goods to little old ladies... whilst Mr Vassell was in the back carving up a cow, waltzing himself to the wafting sounds of classical music. This, amazingly, wasn't the most disturbing thing that happened during my time there.

One Tuesday, I was in the front of the shop, hair net on, ready to serve or talk to anyone who might care to walk in. As you might surmise, it was a slow day. I heard a bit of a kerfuffle in the back by the giant walk-in fridge that held the carcasses. I saw Mr Vassell with his back to me, shoulder shrugged and head down like he was reading a text message. (Of course, he wasn't, still no mobile phones in 1986.)

Then, he turned his head around, back to me and flashed a cheeky-come-sinister grin. His large body slowly turned towards me, his shoulders in perpetual motion. Then I saw what he was up to. For whatever reason, he thought it would be amusing to stick a cut-off ox tongue out of his zipper and do the helicopter with it. Do you know how big an ox's tongue is? It takes a lot of effort, given it's the size of a small leg! Why? Why? Why?

And so, after a total of just two weeks, I resigned with immediate effect. Wouldn't you?

I realise that events may all seem to be happening here in a very linear fashion. However, in reality, many things were happening in parallel, and that's something that still works for me to this day, with a focus on a big-picture item somewhere. In this case, the parallel occurrence was that I had finally passed my driving test, turned 17 years old and managed to get a job that used this new skill. So, I didn't quit the ox tongue helicopter man without having something new lined up.

Introducing Harvey, the delivery driver. Guaranteed an animal-part-free employment opportunity.

Speedy Parts were in the business of same-day delivery of car parts to the trade in the northern part of Stockport. The phone would ring, and exhausts, spark plugs, etc. would be loaded into my tiny 2-door car, and off I'd drive to small local garages, dropping them off. I had to do just two things:

1. Make sure the right parts went to the right place in time, and
2. Make sure the paperwork gets signed.

For a (short) period, this job worked for me. I (still!) had no clue what I wanted to do. It was a low-friction gig where I could listen to the radio all day long, drive by myself, and no one could bother me. There were no mobile phones, no Internet, and no GPS tracking. So, I'd drive the 'circuit' 2–3 times a day, depending on order volumes on the day.

Radio blasting BBC Radio One, window down, cigarette in hand. I was ignoring the speed limits. Ah, that last bit was a bit of a problem.

Turns out, when you drive double the speed limit, and smoke cigarettes whilst punching the air to Bon Jovi on the radio, the risks of a traffic accident are somewhat heightened. And then realised. Smack into the back of a stationary vehicle! Which seemed to hardly have a scratch on it whilst my little old delivery vehicle was a total write-off.

Given how fast I was driving, it was a miracle that no one was hurt. So, I stopped at a pay phone and went to ring the office. The call went something like this.

"Hello, Speed Parts."

"Hello, it's Harvey."

"Yes, Harvey."

"I've had a bit of an accident in the car. Can you come and pick me up?"

"What kind of accident?"

"Err... the car's not drivable, I need someone to come get me."

"F&*^%! Where are you?"

"I'm in New Mills on the main road."

"We're coming."

When they saw the wreck on the street, the car was in such a state that they had to tow it back to the office. Even though the vehicle looked like a squashed tin can, I didn't get fired. What happened was *much* worse than getting fired! They gave me a 15-year-old Yugo car to do the job instead.

A Yugo was a less-than-1000cc vehicle that was the former Yugoslavia's contribution to the global automotive industry. A contribution that the world could have lived without. Like a Trabant that travelled outside of its natural habitat of East Germany. Only worse.

So, I drove it. It had no radio, so the soundtrack of my day was listening to an engine that sounded like it came out of a 20-year-old lawnmower and a gearbox that couldn't find any of its own gears. I crashed it too but not from speeding. Speeding was impossible in a Yugo. I crashed it because I couldn't stop it without a 20-minute warning as the brakes were so bad.

Six weeks of working at Speedy Parts had yielded two written-off cars and a demotion. Although I take no responsibility for the Yugo.

My demotion lasted 30 minutes because I quit. That was the

only job I ever quit without having another job to go to. I'm not a quitter. But I wasn't willing to spend any of my time stacking pre-owned tyres either, which is what Speedy Parts wanted me to do, spending all my time in a dirty industrial hanger.

I was 17, getting on the bus to go home and out of work. Again. And no closer to knowing what I want to do.

Or was I?

KEY LESSONS IN LIFE AND BUSINESS

LEARN HOW TO CONDUCT YOURSELF

From leaving school to going to my first job, I thought I could behave the same, which got me fired.

It remains the only job I've ever been fired from.

Honestly, I deserved to get fired. I swore at a customer, and I was horrible. I used to smoke on the shop floor and was utterly unprepared for the world of work. **I had to learn how to conduct myself in the workplace.**

Everyone has to learn this lesson, and I see it when graduates join a company; they're like rabbits in headlights. They're like, 'What is this place?' And then you say, 'You own this project. You've got to deliver it,'... and they run to the toilet every 10 minutes in a panic. They've got a boss, they're expected to deliver commercial results, and there are consequences for not doing it.

Learning about the transition to the workplace is not as smooth and easy as people think. All of a sudden, you have real responsibility for the first time in your life. Responsibility to the business, responsibility to the customers, and responsibility to yourself.

THERE IS ALWAYS SOMETHING AT STAKE

Marks & Spencer was my Dad's place of work. He might not have been in the same branch, **but I couldn't fuck up.** It was that simple. He must have been nervous, but I think I did him proud. I was trained properly, there were expectations, and they taught me how to meet them. At the end of the day, I only lost out on a permanent position because of my long hair – which would never happen today.

SOMETIMES YOU GET COMFORTABLE

Working for a big company like Marks & Spencer can make you feel comfortable and cushioned, as there's strength in numbers. One person's strength is another person's weakness, and vice versa. So, when you all pull together, it's just one homogenous effort, right? Whereas when you're working in a company of five people like I was at Speedy Parts, there's nowhere to hide.

Looking back, I quit Speedy Parts and the butcher's job because I came out of the comfort zone and structure of Marks & Spencer. It was a huge culture shock going from a big national institution, which was quite warm and nurturing, to ending up working in a deli with a butcher, doing the helicopter with an ox tongue in his pants.

CHAPTER 3

THANK YOU FOR THE MUSIC

"**R**eturn ticket to Arden Sixth Form College, please!" I said, grinning at the bus driver like the Cheshire Cat. Today was the day I was going to change everything. I was going to take my first steps to do what I cared about, loved and wanted to dedicate myself to. No longer would I do crappy jobs and waste my time. I was determined to work in music, and a recording studio course at Arden Sixth Form College was the launch pad I needed.

I had spent months trying to break into the music industry with no success. I had lost count of the number of doors that were slammed into my face. I was Harvey from Manchester, and there were very limited options. I wrote to *all* of the established Manchester-based music companies, visited studios, spoke to the music community, and it became clear I had to specialise. I had to find my niche.

What part of the music business did I want to be in? The creative process, the culture of the studio environment, and the technical aspect fuelled my curiosity. That was it. The recording studio was for me!

Having the desire and focus to know what you want is only a

part of the story; having no technical expertise was the glaring hole in my storyline. So, I had to have a place to start.

Manchester had three options: two were costly private studio courses, and one was an officially qualified course at a local college.

Arden Sixth Form College, now The Manchester College, was the only recognised educational establishment with a qualified course for the music industry in Manchester in 1987. It was a two-year Higher National Diploma (HND) in Popular Music and Sound Recording. And the college had a brand-new recording studio.

I went to the prospectus open day, heard about the course, saw the facility, and it was all good. And then learnt that I was under qualified to get on the two-year HND course. My school education (or lack thereof) had come to well and truly bite me on the arse. My world ended before it started.

But, if there's one thing I've learned over the years, I usually find a way to make things happen despite the odds or circumstances.

After the open day, my disappointment riding over me, I sought the course tutor out. He was a decent guy, he listened as I told him my story of playing in bands, being driven by music and my desire to work in the industry. He saw a drive and passion in me. He excused himself, but little did I know that he went to speak to the principal at the college. When he returned, he found me in the main engineer's chair, coveting the recording console. Dreaming.

He had a plan. He told me that there was a night school version of the course each Wednesday, and if I completed the night school course successfully, the college principal would accept that as an 'access course' to my application to get on to the two-year HND course, a year later. So, I needed to wait a year, do night school, and then I'd get what I wanted.

I grasped the opportunity with both hands and started night

school in September. It wasn't so much a foot on the ladder but a big toe, but I didn't care. For the first time, I could see the path ahead, and I felt good about it.

However, there was one major flaw in the plan. Night school was only three hours a week for a year. My days would be long and empty. My parents were less than thrilled about me bumming around for a year, so I decided to become a volunteer for Outreach after my mum had made a connection with someone she knew.

Outreach was a charity-funded organisation that took young people with special needs into social environments to help give their parents or carers a break. As a volunteer, my role was to help out by going on trips and helping the kids in social situations.

Some of these 'social situations' were a little hairy. When I saw one of the kids trying to strangle our bus driver (whilst he was driving) and one carving his name in the green paint of a restaurant door with his teeth, I realised this was more of a challenge than it seemed – nonetheless, a worthy one.

I learnt a lot about compassion, patience, and empathy during the year I volunteered. I had no idea that over 20 years from this moment, this experience would come to serve me well.

So, whilst night school and volunteering took some of my time, there were no money-making endeavours. I was still playing in a rock band at this point, hair getting longer and guitars getting louder. Then randomly, one day, the lead singer asked me if I wanted to help him work on the weekend. He worked for a concert sound hire company in Manchester, and one of their regular clients, who were famous in the 1960s, was doing gigs up and down the country.

The pitch at our band practice was, "Want to come to help me on Saturday night with the band for £5 and a bag of chips?" Even in the 1980s, that was nothing.

"Yeah, OK!" Where's the gig?" I replied.

Margate Winter Gardens was a five-hour drive from home and 275 miles, but as with all these 'jobs', it was a same-night round trip, so ten hours driving, 550 miles and a gig and a bag of chips in-between.

The long hours on the road in a dilapidated, cold rent-a-wreck van were the hardest part. The gig itself was easy. Unload a van of large amounts of heavy musical equipment, schlep it, set it up, the show comes and goes, tear it all down, schlep it again, load the van, and drive back.

Welcome to the world of being a roadie!

At this point, I was looking the part as well. My hair had become long in the era of 'Big Hair Rock Bands', and I was equipped with a mini-Maglite torch and a tool kit for guitars. I looked like I lived the rock and roll life. Then went back to Mum and Dad's house.

From the back, my sister and I must have looked the same because one day, sitting next to each other on a bus, I got a tap on the shoulder from a little old lady.

"Excuse me, ladies," she said, "do you have the time?"

I turned around slowly and said slightly deeper than expected, "Yes, darlin', it's ten past three." And I gave her a big cheesy grin – Billy Connolly style. I think the beard was the giveaway as I took a mental picture of the look of abject horror on her face. I think she missed her stop!

Back to Margate Winter Gardens. After quite a gruelling drive, we had to go to work. I was ready to go to sleep (already!). When you get to a venue, you look for the 'load in', somewhere to park and get the shortest schlep for the kit.

On arrival, I soon found myself on stage. The venue was a decent size, held approximately 1,000 people, and was an example of a somewhat bygone era. Winter Garden venues were typically for tea dances, children's pantomimes, and inoffensive events.

They weren't for long-haired rockers from Manchester. The band we worked for were not long-haired rockers. I had more hair than all of them put together. Herman's Hermits were hugely popular in the mid-1960s. So popular that one year they were bigger than The Beatles and were a massive part of the British invasion of America.

This was my introduction to the revival circuit. In the 1960s, 1970s and 1980s, bands all played their hits to audiences who reminisced. On the bill that first night in Margate was:

- Herman's Hermits.
- The Searchers (not sure which version).
- Someone else from the 1960s, I can't remember. Sorry.

When I state 'not sure which version,' this refers to a very specific dynamic in legacy artists, especially from the 1960s and 1970s. Often, there were bitter breakups and legal in-fighting, and sometimes, as a consequence, members of a famous band would not speak to each other for years or even forever. I've worked with and alongside bands where there were at least two versions of the same band. Often, the names were subtly different for legal reasons and usually had just one or two original members in each band.

I knew of one well-known band with NO original members working on the circuit. I wonder how many people paid to see them without realising. I thought that was verging on fraud, but what do I know?

There was much bitterness with some of the bands. The more you got to know them and learned their stories, the more you realised how exploited some of them had been during their window of fame. When you toured with them, you'd hear the full details, and some of the stories were shocking.

Unfortunately, many of these bands were still working years

or decades later because they had to. They were not equal stakeholders in their previous success, and the cheques and balances that are the established 'norms' these days were simply non-existent in their time.

The 'Hermits' were on stage joking about when we arrived. "Where the fuck have you been?" said Lek, was the riposte, delivered with a cheeky smile.

"This is Harvey," said my friend, "he's helping out."

I gave them a slightly awkward acknowledgement that that was me.

The van doors creaked open so badly that I thought they'd fall off before the night was over. Over the next few weeks, things would fall off the van that weren't supposed to, but the doors, by some miracle, stayed on. Can you imagine if they'd fallen off whilst we were driving? A ton or two of musical equipment all over the road at speed?

So, we lugged the kit in... I thought Led Zeppelin or Black Sabbath were playing, judging by how much equipment there was. I knew nothing, the amount of backline kit (drums, guitar amps, etc.) was relatively light, but when there were only two of you, and there were stairs involved in the 'load in', it was backbreaking work. When multiple flights of stairs were involved, the feeling of getting it over with would be front and centre of the whole gig.

In Margate, I just followed the orders as they got barked out. Put that flight case here, put that drum case there, I learnt the stage layout for the band in 10 minutes. Each band has their own stage plan, and The Hermits' was very simple. The challenge with this kind of multi-band bill is the 'change over', swapping all the kit from one band to another and trying to get it set up and sounding like it was at sound check in the afternoon. I can't remember when it went perfectly, I can remember times when it didn't! There certainly was an art to it, upon which the basics were founded on marking every position and setting with Duct Tape and a Chinagraph pencil.

The kit for a roadie was his lifeblood (plus chips, gravy, and beer). The essentials list, as I quickly learnt, was as follows:

1. Duct tape, aka. gaffa tape. Stick everything, especially extraneous cables, and mark everything's position on the floor.
2. Chinagraph pencil. Mark settings on amps and sound boards, and write notes.
3. Mini-Maglite torch. See everything. When the lights go out, you are blind on stage while crawling around on your hands and knees, trying to fix something.
4. Guitar strings and clippers. Because the guitar player has fingers like jumbo sausages and the dexterity of an elephant, you need to be ready to change a string or two, usually midway through his best-known song! Where's the spare guitar?
5. Guitar string winder. See 4.
6. Bottle opener. Because some of the bands you will work with will be alcoholics. Or worse, you need to help them flip the lid off a brew whilst they are eyeing the blond divorcee in the front row, mid-song. Bless, they only have two hands, and at least one of them is on the guitar.
7. Belt with clips. Because like a mountain climber, you'll never know when you'll need to attach yourself to something, or something will need to get connected to you. You, too, only have two hands; sometimes, you'll hang from a lighting rig or stand on a tower of speakers more prominent than your (parents') house.
8. Bum bag (aka. fanny pack if you are in the USA). Are you really going to carry all of the above?

Over time and as the gig count went up, I'd sit front-of-house during sound check and watch and listen. I'd ask questions, and sooner rather than later, I'd get my fingers on the sound desk under supervision. Usually, if my bandmate had to go to the stage and do something, I stood guard on the desk. I loved the feeling of control, shaping the sound the audience would hear.

My friend would explain the basics to me, and with my night schooling, I learned the similarities and differences between the soundboards in the studio and the ones for live shows. In fact, in the 1980s and before computers and automation became standardised, there was not much difference to me for most of it.

It didn't happen often, but if the band you were working for was opening the show, you were last to sound check, which meant you didn't have to move anything until it was time to go home or go to the bar.

Killing time was hard sometimes. Especially if you had long drives behind and ahead of you. After sound check in the afternoon, typically around 3pm, you'd have at least six hours to kill with nothing to do until show time. What do you do in Margate (or the like) for six hours?

The usual thing would be to go for something to eat. And it was during this time that I developed a taste for Indian food. Quite often, after soundcheck, there'd be a treasure hunt for the best Indian restaurant or takeaway in the area and then a competition to see who could eat the spiciest food.

Experiencing 'Delhi belly' during a show was a common experience. The drive home would often be, how can I say, anti-social.

So, this show came and went without an incident. What I do remember is the overwhelming feeling of exhaustion. By the time the band walked on stage, I was ready for bed. But, we had a one-hour show, followed by tearing the kit down, packing up, schlepping the gear, packing the van and then the worst part. 275-mile drive home through the night in a rent-a-wreck van.

We made staying awake an art form. I had a few basic tactics:

I drove for as long as I could before introducing any other measure.

1. Listen to the radio
2. Open a window for fresh air
3. Smoke a cigarette with the window slightly open
4. Drink a coffee, sometimes with a cigarette
5. Take a Pro Plus tablet. These were caffeine tablets that were legal 'stay awake' pills
6. Stop for 10 minutes if I had to, walk about, and hit myself in the face

When I got to step six, my only option on really long drives was to go back to step three and repeat steps three-six. Sometimes, I'd be so wired when I got back to Manchester around 4am that going to sleep wasn't easy.

For a year, I took night school, volunteered at Outreach and spent most weekends in a van cutting my teeth as a roadie. I enjoyed night school a lot, I learned that I felt comfortable, curious and engaged in this environment. My time volunteering had been unforgettable, thanks to the people I had met and the personal stories I had heard. And I was getting busier travelling up and down the country, honing my roadie skills. Much busier.

But then the critical moment came and went without much friction. I got accepted onto the Higher National Diploma course for Popular Music and Sound Recording. My next two years were mapped out ahead of me.

KEY LESSONS IN LIFE AND BUSINESS

YOU'VE GOT TO PUT WORK INTO A FOCUS AREA

When I was unemployed, I realised that I needed to put work into a focus area that was meaningful for me. I wasn't on a career path to becoming a doctor or lawyer. I needed to find my own way, so I got on the bus and headed for college because I wanted to get into music.

THERE WILL BE CHALLENGES YOU HAVE TO OVERCOME

I wanted to enrol on the course but couldn't because I had no qualifications. I had to find a way to make it happen. **My passion had to open the door for me.**

At work, I often find ways to make things happen in a way that other people don't. I'd say it's one of my strengths, and it started here.

WIDENING YOUR PERSPECTIVE IS SO IMPORTANT

We all look at the world through a very narrow lens of our own life. We're just not exposed to how many other people live in this world. You can widen your perspective by travelling and learning new things, they're all nice things to do. But many people in this world live with challenges they didn't ask for, like the parents of the young people who attended Outreach.

I would encourage you to volunteer to help someone who needs it, even if it's just a few hours a month, do it. It's good for your soul.

I didn't appreciate it at the time, but now I know, through family circumstances, how much respite carers are needed and the impact they have. If your company allows you to do a charity day, make sure you take it and do something. Learn something about yourself and others. Whether that's helping people with special needs or being a porter for a day in a hospital. Go to a care home and listen to the residents' stories of yesterday. It matters.

YOU NEED A CHAMPION

You can't do everything yourself; sometimes, you need a champion to help you. My champion was my tutor at college, who found a way to get me on the course. Without him, my life would have turned out very different, and I wouldn't be here now.

I've sometimes played the role of champion in companies, whether that's championing people to get them hired, championing them on specific projects, or celebrating them.

You need to get someone to champion you. Buddy up with someone and get mentored. When you get championed, you'll grow exponentially, and it'll help you grease the passage of progress. You won't be facing an uphill struggle.

CHAPTER 4

FEELS LIKE HEAVEN

"**H**arvey," my tutor called out. "You will be spending your work experience at... Moonraker Studios!"

I couldn't believe it. I'd been expecting to be sent to the ballet or the flippin' opera or something else inappropriate for a genuine rock poodle. There weren't many real working recording studios in Manchester, but I'd struck gold.

I knew of Moonraker Studios. Moreover, I knew who owned it. He was famous.

Mike Harding was a well-known Mancunian singer, songwriter and comedian in Britain at the time. He was a familiar face on national TV and the owner of Moonraker Studios. I was to be his tape op(erator) and general dogsbody (a bona fide job in a recording studio) for the next two weeks.

I couldn't wait. The critical construct of the HND course was a diverse grounding based on the studio world. This meant, first and foremost, learning to be a sound engineer, learning an instrument, learning to read music, and basic music business practices. It was quite a generalist course with a heavy lean towards the recording studio. And I'd thrown myself into it. Being in an actual commercial recording studio, though, was going to be something else.

37

I couldn't wait to share my exciting news with my own band. We rehearsed twice a week but performed rarely. I won't share our name (due to fears of high embarrassment). We'd started looking, if not sounding, the part, so much so we managed to get our photo into the weekly Rock bible 'Kerrang!'. I had the almost perfect 'rock poodle' look of the era. Before you try to guess, the band was NOT called Rock Poodle. It was much worse.

Music was my life. There was nothing else, no room for anything else: music college, own band, roadie. I had very little money, but I was happy.

I rolled up on my first day at Moonraker Studios, grinning from ear to ear, wearing denim, leather, and cowboy boots. I thought I looked the dog's bollocks. I was buzzed into the building, promptly ignored for 30 minutes, and then ushered into a dark lair with a myriad of flashing lights. I was in the control room.

Tape op was the bottom rung of the ladder and a genuine step to get to be a recording engineer. It's where most engineers started in those days, as it gave you the technical and cultural grounding you needed if you had any aspiration of progressing.

It wasn't that long ago that everything was recorded to analogue tape before the digital tape came along, then to be overtaken by the digital revolution, which meant computers, automation, and hard disc storage took over.

So, what did I have to do? In simple terms, I had to maintain and clean the tape machine, ensure the tapes were all catalogued effectively, put the tapes on and take the tapes off the recording machine, and 'splice'. Splicing effectively cuts the tape, sometimes to remove some erroneous audio and stick it back together. It's basically tape surgery whilst walking the highwire. One wrong cut and the band would lose their recordings. Forever.

All this aside, 95% of my time (and any tape op's time) is spent sitting at the outside edge of the recording console, where the producer and leading engineer would sit in the middle, and you press the red record button. And the stop button.

Often routine and desperately dull, your skills would get tested on drop-ins. A drop-in would be where an artist needed to 'drop in' a vocal or guitar line, often at a critical moment in the song, to ensure you rescued a take or added something extra. You needed twitchy fingers, razor-sharp senses and to be quick on the draw.

The more critical the recording, the more a drop-in would be like a duel at noon. Fingers on triggers, waiting for the crucial moment. Here comes the artist, I'm watching him like a hawk... he opens his mouth and... hits...

RECORD!

(split second goes by...)

STOP!

"OK," I'd say, "we're out." Then the silence. Everyone in the studio would look at each other, wondering if I got it. Then, playback. I'd rewind the tape machine and hit PLAY.

And I'd wait, wait for the moment of the drop-in to see if I captured it cleanly. No one would notice that I'd effectively put a virtual sticking plaster over the recording.

Success would bring a sense of celebration and high fives all-round if it were a very tricky drop-in. I would get the credit, pats on the back, and a general sense of relief.

Failure would sometimes mean discussions with the producer. Do the band have to re-record a whole take? Do we leave whatever it was we were trying to fix? Should we smoke a cigarette and try again?

Studio days were often very long and always dark. There's no outside light in the main studio area, and it's an acoustically optimised area that prioritises how sound is treated, recorded, and heard. Windows are reflective and change the sound, the sound has many other environmental considerations, but that's a different book.

Mike himself was different in the studio to the public persona that I knew. Far more serious when on studio duty. It was business. I seemed to do OK, despite my drop-in skills being average. What was highly valuable was experiencing all this in the real world.

I was given enough responsibility too. I fully managed the tape machines, cataloguing the 2" tape stock and the day-to-day operation of the recording functions. Also known as pushing the buttons.

But it did turn monotonous after a while.

The two weeks flew by and each day and recording session blurred into the next one, and before I knew it, I was back at college.

The lessons came and went. The part I loved the most was sitting in the engineer's chair; the bit I hated the most was learning to read music. I found I had a natural flair for the business side which would serve me well in the not-so-distant future.

Being in the engineer's chair was empowering. The fact that you were a large part of the collective creative process and applied technical know-how to get the desired creative results felt like a type of alchemy to me. When you heard something that sounded great over the speakers you know you helped shape, it was very satisfying.

Over the next few months, the college became somewhat routine partly because the demand for studio time was high. All of the students wanted to be in the studio all the time because, like me, that was the main attraction of the course.

Some students had very little intention of fulfilling a career in music. For some, it was a way to pass the time and get a more interesting qualification than a STEM-based subject.

For some, it was a way to get a cheap demo tape, but for me, it was because I had a deadly serious objective.

I did start feeling a bit bored at college, but I didn't let my focus waver. I had to stick with it.

In the 1980s, there was no college course to learn how to be a roadie or find a career in touring. You got in any way you could. You might've worked for an audio company that hired out touring sound systems, and you'd go with it. You might have worked for a concert trucking or logistics company. You might've been a rock poodle in a local band in Manchester whose lead singer worked for a local PA (sound) hire company, and you'd work for £5 and a bag of chips.

What happened next was utterly unexpected. My roadie career was about to take on a new twist… and I needed to get a (temporary) passport.

KEY LESSONS IN LIFE AND BUSINESS

MAKE A COMMITMENT

I needed to practice being good at something and became a roadie outside of college. It was about cutting my teeth early and paying my dues. I learnt so much.

Being 100% committed is so important. It meant I was working and studying music as much as possible.

DON'T LOSE SIGHT OF THE BIG PICTURE

When college started to get boring, I could've thrown in the towel, but I didn't. I saw the benefit of completing the course and completing what I'd worked so hard for.

Sometimes life and work can be boring. You can go through a period of being discouraged and bored at work, but the key is staying focused on the big picture and the ultimate destination you've set for yourself.

It's normal to be bored now and again; it's part of the journey. However, it's important to focus on your final destination and navigate the challenges you may face along the way.

THE KINGSWAY SCHOOL

Headmaster   George J Nicholls   JP BSc Econ Dip Man Ed

UPPER SCHOOL

Foxland Road
Cheadle Cheshire SK8 4QA

Telephone 061-428 7706 4990

LOWER SCHOOL

High Grove Road
Cheadle Cheshire SK8 1NP

Telephone 061-428 2759 7850

Headmaster's Report on   HARVEY ANTHONY LEE

Date of Admission   September 1979   Date of Leaving   June 1984

GRADINGS :	A - Very Good	B - Good	C - Average/Satisfactory
	D - Slightly below average		E - Poor

ATTENDANCE: Very Good   PUNCTUALITY: Excellent

ACADEMIC ATTAINMENT: O Level Course (O)   C.S.E. Course (CS)

Studies in depth

ENGLISH LANGUAGE (CS)	–	C	GEOGRAPHY (16+)	–	D/E
MATHEMATICS (CS)	–	C	PHYSICS (16+)	–	E
TECHNICAL DRAWING (O,CS)	–	C	ECONOMICS (O)	–	D
CHEMISTRY (CS)	–	E			

BASIC COURSE

In addition, Harvey   has completed a Basic Course of three years'
duration covering literacy, numeracy, social studies, a foreign language,
science studies, religious education, music, technical/craft studies, art,
physical education and social and personal development.

CHARACTER AND PERSONALITY

Attitude to work	E	Sociability	B
Perseverance	D	Courtesy	D
Initiative	C	Personal appearance	B
Other characteristics	Honest, reliable.		

Further remarks :   Harvey has not reaped the benefits of the opportunities
available to him.   He has been far too easily satisfied with his efforts and often
gives up when difficulties are encountered.   Unfortunately his often lethargic
attitude has not helped his progress.

However, Harvey does get on well with others, particularly those who have a real
interest in rock music.   Harvey plays the guitar and writes songs.

16th May, 1984.   *George Nicholls.*

▲ I received my school leaving report in 1984. Despite there
being no silver lining, the comments at the end provided
valuable hints about my future.

◄ This throwback photo of me was taken on my first day of school, way back in 1973. Interestingly, Angus Young from AC/DC would start sporting the same outfit on stage just a year later in 1974. Oh, the irony!

► Age 15, playing my second gig at the Boars Head pub in Stockport. I chose to play bass guitar because it only had four strings. Given my musical limitations, it's possible that the bass guitar chose me!

◄ Things are getting serious. By age 17 I was at music college, a weekend roadie, and competently playing in a band. And even had a photo featured in rock bible, *KERRANG!*

CHAPTER 5

(WE ARE) THE ROADCREW

"Harvey! Make sure you sell a full box of T-shirts tonight so you can eat next week!" shouted Lek, guitarist and leader of Herman's Hermits. Not very subtle, but the message and urgency were understood.

No longer in Margate Winter Gardens – we were gigging in Germany, Denmark and Norway. The touring format was low-budget. The band would drive themselves in a hire car, while we, the two and only members of the roadcrew, would do what we usually did back home, only *far* from home.

The scenery might've changed, but unfortunately, the van and the kit we had to schlep around Europe didn't. There weren't hundreds of miles to do anymore, but thousands – in the same rent-a-rust-bucket of a vehicle.

We were in Gelsenkirchen, Germany. The Hermits had played their set, and the luxury for me was that there was no equipment to take down or pack. But I did have to sell T-shirts.

Merchandising was vital to the band's income at these shows, so much so that I learned that my very modest wages depended on good sales. And the band had no problem in letting me know that.

At this gig, there was a merchandising table set up for all the bands to share, with a percentage of the sales going to the house as a concession. The table was in a dark corner with inferior access for the audience with non-existent signposting. No one was selling anything. Not one T-shirt. And all of the bands and their roadcrews were complaining.

After The Hermits show, back in the dressing room, the band were in an expectant mood on the merchandising 'take' after doing reasonably well on the previous shows. But I had news.

"Sorry, lads, it's awful out there; no one's selling anything," I told them.

The news was received with a look of murderous intent. With me as the victim.

"Er, hold on... I've got an idea... give me 15 minutes..."

I knew the problem, it wasn't hard to work it out. The real issue was that no one was doing anything, and no one was taking action to remediate the situation. The other bands just accepted it.

The venue, a large sports arena, was still full of thousands of people. They were tapping their feet, clapping their hands, and chewing on a giant pretzel or bratwurst. Here, I thought, was *the* captive audience, and they wanted to spend even more money to remember what a great night out they had had.

They just didn't know it yet!

So, I loaded up two armfuls of Herman's Hermits T-shirts in mixed sizes and hit the seating area. I thought, if the audience weren't coming to the merchandising table, I'd go to them!

I'm pretty sure that I broke all the house rules by walking up the aisles, shouting "Herman's Hermits T-Shirts!"

By holding them above my head, I got a reaction. The kind of reaction that saw us sell half our total inventory and fill our pockets with Deutsche Marks (it was 1988, people, the Euro didn't exist yet). The audience, whether full of beer and brat or not, was in the mood, and they parted with their cash wilfully.

The band knew something was up when I kept returning to the dressing room for more T-shirts. They thought I was done the first time, and we'd done OK. After the sixth time, they couldn't quite believe their eyes. Or pocketbooks.

Lek was so happy he started doing a merry jig, singing made-up songs about making *so much* money.

"We got the Shekels, we got the Shekels!" he sang.

And then I was 'awarded' my new nickname.

From that moment onwards, I was known in the music business in Manchester as The Shekel. Or just Shekel for short. The name stuck so much that when I made a phone call, I had to use my new moniker, as no one knew who 'Harvey' was!

I'd make a call, and it'd go like this, "Can I speak to Derek, please?"

"Who is it?"

"It's Harvey."

"Who?"

"It's Shekel."

"Ah, Shekel, hold on, Shek, I'll get him."

Yes, it got so truncated from The Shekel to Shekel, to Shek that it was only a matter of time before I would be known as S (symbol), the roadie formerly known as Shekel!

I was having a whale of a time, and I was only 19. I'd hardly left Britain before, so this was a huge adventure. The days of £5 wages and a bag of chips were gone.

I still laugh to myself when I look at my passport from back then (yes, I still have the original). In 1988, you were allowed to wear glasses in passport photos and coats. My passport photo was close to full Rocker mode, with longish big hair and tinted-shaded glasses.

I didn't half-clock up some miles that spring. It took us over

24 hours to make it to Bremen, Germany alone, and that gig was my first outdoor festival.

It was in the city centre square near the central train station and was a cracker of a gig. Big stage, plenty of help, and lots of sausages! There were wooden stalls around the square, and I swear every other booth was selling some sort of sausage too.

It was a free gig, and no one paid to see the bands. Old buildings enclosed the square, and thousands of people were there, full of sausage and German beer. There was a great atmosphere; everyone in the crowd seemed drunk. Wasted Fräuleins, rowdy Herrs. The band and crowd had a great time during their set.

Honestly, I think you could've put a brown paper bag on a chair on that stage, and the crowd would've cheered for it. So, given that The Hermit's played with an energy I'd not yet seen, it made it that bit more special. It was a far cry from the usual blue rinse brigade they normally played to in the UK.

Another memorable show in Germany attracted crowds of 8,000 plus. The 'revival' circuit for legacy bands in Germany was probably one of the biggest, if not *the* most significant market. So most of the biggest shows were in Germany.

The format was becoming increasingly familiar. Large venue, multi-band bill, an easier day for the roadcrew. This gig featured The Hermits, Gidea Park, and notably, The Sweet. The Sweet were a very big thing in the early 1970s. Very big. Their songs 'Hellraiser', 'Blockbuster', and 'Ballroom Blitz' were part of the decade's soundtrack.

The band had had many incarnations over the years, fallouts, and lawsuits, but somehow *this* version (using the name The New Sweet) was still going. This version of the band featured Brian Connolly, their original lead singer.

This was the first time I witnessed a true victim of rock and roll. This guy was the walking dead, a ghost of his former self.

Too much good partying in his heyday had led to him being addicted to everything that was wrong with the music business.

He could barely stand, let alone hold a conversation. He was constantly shaking, his voice was croaky, and his speech was disjointed. This guy made Ozzy Osbourne look like Usain Bolt!

"He's going to be on stage soon; how's he going to manage that?" I whispered to Barry, The Hermit's drummer.

A few minutes later, I bore witness to Brian being slowly escorted to the stage as he held onto an assistant. He walked as if he was 120 years old and had been sitting down for 40 years! Oh my, there are stairs! Ten minutes to navigate eight steps, and he was on stage!

The lights went out. The crowd got going, and Brian was gently escorted to the microphone stand. He leaned on it for the whole set as if it was his life support system. His feet didn't move for the entire gig, but somehow, he got through it.

I remember after the show, watching him 'recover' in the dressing room, thinking what a tragedy it was that someone who, in the 1970s, was a genuine rock icon could end up this way.

Brian Connolly died in 1997, aged 51, of kidney failure after a life of drinking and repeated health problems, including multiple heart attacks.

We headed to Denmark next, primarily for the band to do some recording at a studio, but we picked up a couple of gigs to help pay for things.

The standout location of all the Danish gigs was Copenhagen. The venue was the Carlsberg Brewery. Literally, the place they make all that beer. But there were major disappointments and challenges.

Not only was the venue tiny, but it was also just a small bar for their staff, and it was pretty empty. The fact that the gig was a bit of a washout wasn't the main issue.

Around this time, the beat-up old Ford van I was travelling

around in was starting to break down at a higher frequency rate. The breakdowns had started as overheating or things we were able to fix ourselves temporarily. But from Copenhagen onwards, the breakdowns were serious. The bloody thing wouldn't start.

We arrived in Copenhagen with the van on the back of a rescue truck and *left* Copenhagen with the van on the back of a rescue truck. It was a pattern we'd have to endure for the rest of the tour.

We did, however, get a one-week break when we arrived at a residential recording studio in Nibe, Denmark.

The band hadn't seen much income from their original sound recordings since their heyday. There were more tales of a music business that helped itself, questionable practices, and legal challenges. Many, I came to learn, would never, ever be resolved.

The Hermits had decided to re-record their biggest hits, using their money to pay for the recordings. This meant, legally, for these recordings, they would own them, and when pressed onto vinyl (it was 1988, people still bought music on physical formats), it'd also give me more inventory to sell at the merchandising table.

The studio, Stuk Ranch, as it was known then, is a very popular and well-known, well-appointed studio. Our job was to load the amps and drums, then we had a few days off to watch the band, the producer they had hired and be general gophers.

The sound mixing desk was enormous, but that wasn't the main feature. They had a 'Fairlight', one of the earliest digital workstations and it was *very* expensive. It was the computer and sound automation tool of the day, and you needed the expertise to use it. It'd turn a drum that sounded like tin pots being hit with twigs into a well-produced pounding beat that even Def Leppard would be proud of.

Compared to the modest studio I was learning in at college, this was some kind of magic.

I sat on the sofa at the back of the control room, watching, listening, and hoping to learn something. And I did... but not what I expected.

The band went out for dinner, got wasted, and then arrived for a recording session in the studio. It was a waste of time creatively. It served only to reveal tensions. Lips got looser, and false courage got bigger.

It was the first time I'd heard about the band's legal struggles and the differing opinions between the original band members. They had been the biggest band in America in 1965, bigger than The Beatles. Yet where was all the money? Years of lawyer meetings had yielded very little.

So, when it got very heated, bitter and resentful, I stood up, half wasted myself, and stopped the tape recorder. It was one thing to play the producer on fart recordings. It was another to have a recording of two former pop stars verbally slugging it out.

The morning after the night before, there was a quiet, reflective atmosphere at breakfast, littered with the occasional verbal jab at one another.

"Pass the jam, you tosser."

"Here you go, twat."

And then, things got back to normal during the recording session. But my life was about to change. And I'd need (another) new but permanent passport.

KEY LESSONS IN
LIFE AND BUSINESS

OBSERVE THE SALES PATTERN

You must recognise when something isn't working and change your sales pattern. I did that when the T-shirts weren't selling. I had the balls to go to direct distribution, walk through the crowd, and sell the flipping things. It's the adage, if the mountain doesn't come to you, you need to go to the mountain. Things weren't going my way, so I had to turn it on its head, but I didn't ask permission.

MAKE A NAME FOR YOURSELF

I gained my nickname, and that part was all fun. However, making a name for yourself in life and business is important. It can open doors and help make things happen. **You need to be remembered for all the right reasons, the attributes you've built for yourself that'll be central to your career positioning.**

In my case, this was getting shit done, making things happen, doing the dirty work, and focusing on the box office and merchandising. This was something my predecessors didn't want to do, yet it was crucial to the band. It became my calling card.

DOING GREAT WORK CONSISTENTLY
FORGES REPUTATION AND REWARD

I didn't find out until 30 years later that the band had deliberated taking 'the kid', as they referred to me, to the USA in the summer of '88.

But that's precisely what happened.

My no-nonsense, get-the-work-done approach had been

noticed. I'd proven to be an effective, valued member of a small, close-knit team. When you work so closely with people for long durations of time away from home, your relationships are everything – in both these regards and the willingness to get my hands dirty catapulted me to the top of the consideration pile.

Whatever your context, you can do great work. If no one sees or knows about it, in terms of perception, it's like it never happened. Seize the opportunity for projects that have significant personal visibility, build your personal brand, and get out of your comfort zone.

The rewards will come. Maybe not immediately, and maybe not in your current job. But they *will* come.

CHAPTER 6

TAKE ON ME

"Hey Shek, what are you doing this summer?" asked Bean as I relaxed on the grass with the band outside the studio. Bean was Barry Whitwam, Herman's Hermits' original drummer.

"Er... nothing much, it's holidays from college," I replied, unsuspectingly.

"How would you like to come to America with us in July for three months?" he replied with a huge shit-eating grin.

I was so shocked that I struggled to get my words out, "Erm... what? Excuse me, what? YES!!!! Er... but what about Jez? He's fully expecting to go."

Bean shrugged, "Leave him to us; we'll talk to him."

All of the band members were looking at me with some sense of welcoming to the fold. They'd found someone they could work with, a spiritual kinship.

"But why me? Why not Jez?" I said, struggling to process what had just happened.

"Shek, we've not known you long, but we've made more of a connection with you. You've shown an understanding of what we care about and that matters to us much more.

"Jez only cares about the technical aspect. Yes, it's important, but we focus on business and the people we get on with. On this tour, we're in each other's pockets, we need a team player," Lek said.

"You've shown us you can get a job done and be flexible. And you never considered the US tour a God-given right. Plus, you sealed the deal in Gelsenkirchen.

"We need to sell **a lot** of T-shirts in America to make up your wages. You're *The Shekel*; there's no better in the business at shifting merchandise."

I was in a daze. Something truly remarkable had happened. I was just 19, and I'd been asked to go on tour to America. We'd be leaving in just a few weeks. I was going to be living my rock and roll dreams. But I knew there was one crucial thing I had to do... I had to let my Mum know.

I set off for the nearest phone box, four miles away. I couldn't use the studio phone because I didn't want to be overheard by Jez. So off I went, walking through the Danish countryside. The sun shone gloriously as I walked by vast fields, winding through narrow country lanes.

Once encapsulated inside the phone booth, I managed to tell my Mum through a mixture of stuttering and verbal splurting; even the weather becoming overcast didn't take any of the shine off.

My parents saw the opportunity too and were very excited for me. It was 1988, and we didn't know anyone who had been to America, let alone travelled to America to work.

By the time I got back to the studio, I was shattered. And soaked. The walk had been longer, more challenging, and much wetter than I'd expected. It was almost as if a black cloud had followed me back from the phone booth. I was still feeling on cloud nine, but it turns out the real black cloud belonged to someone else.

"Judas," Jez spat as he walked past me. With such force, it might as well have been wrapped around a brick and thrown in my face.

My walk to protect him from finding out had been a waste of time. The band must have told him already. Jez knew I was going to the States instead of him. I was no Judas, but he believed what he wanted to believe.

And so, with an American tour in my pocket and a very changed atmosphere in the cabin of rent-a-wreck, we soldiered on with the remainder of the tour.

Next stop, Norway. And jail. Well, technically, it was the customs impound.

Arriving at the port of Kristiansand on the ferry from Denmark, we were met with a sudden and new reality. We didn't have the correct Carnet (customs) documentation to bring the musical equipment into the country.

1988 was before the European Union (EU) existed in its current form, and free movement was, well, not that free. You still needed all the paperwork. Or in our case, the promoter for the Norway shows had to put up a significant bounty of cash as a deposit to get us into the country.

And whilst someone tried to locate him and then convince him to cough up thousands of Kroner (Norway's local currency), our van was impounded by customs and unless the bounty was paid, there would be no show, which meant no money.

The band drove off to the show, which was hours away by road.

Whilst we waited for the promoter to sort things out with customs, we went for a walk. And I learnt the hard way that Norway was one of the most expensive places on earth! £6 ($10) for a beer. In 1988! We drank that beer so carefully and slowly that you'd have thought we were handling a vase from the Ming Dynasty.

And so, with half a very expensive beer in each of our bellies, we sauntered back to the customs impound where the van was being held. And customs were on the phone with the Promoter when we got there.

He didn't want to pay the bond for two reasons. It was a lot of money, even by Norwegian standards, and more importantly, he wouldn't get it back if any of us did anything to get into trouble with the authorities. Like bands do.

But Jez might not have cared about selling T-shirts, but he was good at getting in people's faces. And one unsuspecting concert promoter was about to get his face ripped off over the phone.

Ten minutes later, we pulled out of the customs impound, and we were on our way to Oslo. The band was 12 hours ahead of us. We eventually pulled into the hotel. Amazingly, without the help of a vehicle rescue service.

The next morning, we made up for not being able to afford to eat much the day before whilst at the pleasure of Norwegian customs. The hotel staff witnessed what must have seemed like two large shaggy wild dogs on the rampage through the restaurant, eating anything in their path.

Once satisfied, the band, horrified (but forgiving), sent us on our way to the only gig we were doing in Norway. It must've paid well because it was a hell of a trek for just one show.

The views were incredible. Driving alongside mountain edges, with the water below on our right-hand side and even Jez was being civilised again. The mountain air, crisp and fresh... until...

"Jez, I don't feel very well, I think I might be sick," I mumbled.

"I can't stop the van now, we're going uphill. I'll never get it back up to 30mph again," Jez replied.

Yes, the van really was that bad. If you had momentum, you had to make the best of it.

"Stick your head out of the window, just be careful with the wire coat hanger," Jez ordered.

Slam! Bang! The window fell into the door frame. "Argh!

Harvey that'll be a right pain to fix," Jez was seriously pissed off. Again.

I heard nothing, I was only concerned with what was about to defy gravity. My breakfast!

As Jez wasn't stopping the van, I had no choice. Head out the window, looking to the rear to avoid any 'blowback' and…

BAARRFF!!! BAARRFF!!! BAARRFF!!!

A technicolour yawn covered half the van's side, single-handedly changing its base colour from royal blue to something more psychedelic. I hadn't considered the car behind us that got a good 'splat!'. I just hoped they had plenty of screenwash in their tank.

But that wasn't all. Not by a long way.

"Stop the van!" I demanded.

"I told you I can't!" he retorted.

"It's my stomach, you really have to, I've got another problem…."

Too late.

I closed my eyes; I clenched my teeth and squeezed my buttocks. But it wasn't enough, not by a long way. And then it happened… the **almighty release in my pants!**

That's right. I shit myself in the Norwegian fjords. In a van on my way to a gig. And we were absolutely in the middle of nowhere, with only mountain animals and a clear blue sky for company.

"I can't believe what you've just done. We're miles away from being able to stop anywhere; it's a single lane around this mountain. It's just the goats and us!" Jez shook his head with disgust and despair.

So, with the fresh smell and taste of puke in my mouth and a freshly filled pair of pants, I just had to grin and bear it until we found a place to stop 45 minutes later. If that wasn't bad enough, because of all the problems we'd been having with the van, we had had to have the heating on full blast all the time to keep the heat away from the engine so it did not overheat (again).

Warm puke and shit. Lovely.

We pulled over at a tiny petrol station. It had just one fuel pump. I gently peeled myself from the van's passenger seat and slowly and carefully squelched myself towards the small building of the station. My suitcase was buried in the truck amongst tons of musical equipment, meaning changing wasn't an option. The only option I had was to take my clothes off and attempt to get as clean as possible. There were no showers, but I was grateful for running cold water and electricity.

The only saving grace I had was that the outside of my trousers were largely OK. Twenty minutes later, we were back in the van and on our way up a Norwegian Mountain. At 5 miles an hour.

When we finally got to the gig, the theme of being in the middle of nowhere was maintained. It was some outdoor farmers' convention, agricultural equipment was everywhere, new tractors, hay bales and lord knows what.

Technically speaking, the set-up for the band was reasonable. There was a good stage, a good sound system, and a helpful crew, but we got there so late that I had no time to clean up. So, we threw open the backdoors of the van and just got on with it.

After all that effort, endurance, and challenges, the band played to barely anybody. The audience was literally 20 farmers and some mountain goats. But I didn't care; it was the last date on tour, so the following day, we were going home in clean clothes.

The band had elected to fly home. This left Jez and me with two vehicles to drive back from Oslo to Manchester. The 1,200 km took us 46 hours, 22 hours of solid driving and 24 hours on the ferry. He drove the band's hire car in the relative comfort of heating and air-conditioning and a mechanically sound vehicle. I drove rent-a-wreck.

In a way, despite the challenges of the vehicle, it was a time to reflect. The near non-stop drive took in all the countries we'd been through over the two weeks within two days – Norway, Denmark, Germany, and then back to the UK.

Sure, I sometimes had to hold the window up with my elbow. But the next tour would start with a Boeing 747 to New York. I was confident wire coat hangers would not be holding up the windows on that.

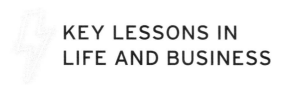

KEY LESSONS IN LIFE AND BUSINESS

REPEATABLE PROCESSES DRIVE TANGIBLE VALUE

Once I had the T-shirt concept sorted in Europe and I was doing the merchandising, we had a repeatable process. The band said, "Well, we've toured America before, but we've never sold this amount of stuff." It cemented my position with the band, as they could see 'this guy's valuable. Not only can he run all the sound stuff, but he can make his money and pay his own wages.'

In a way, I'd like to think my contributions during my career paid my own wages in many organisations I've worked for. When the Xbox Bundle King was born during my time at Microsoft, I took repeatable processes to a whole other level, but more about that later.

UNDERSTAND YOUR VALUE – BUT BE HUMBLE

I knew I was doing a good job with the band from the way they engaged with me. However, unlike my co-worker, I never assumed anything, never took anything for granted, and didn't expect to be asked to go to America.

Maybe I've been too humble sometimes in the past, assuming

my work was seen and valued when it wasn't, but one thing has been consistent: I've stayed true to myself. Make sure you stay true to yourself too.

CHAPTER 7

NEW YORK, NEW YORK

"**D**on't worry, Mrs Lee, I'm sure Harvey will have an experience of a lifetime," said Leonie, the wife of the band leader, Lek. She took a sip of tea and smiled at my mum.

I was feeling very nervous. The band had already flown over, and the plan was for me to fly to New York by myself and then make my way over to the East Coast and meet up with the guys in Providence, Rhode Island. My mum was having second thoughts, and I was due to fly in three days.

"Please don't worry, the band will look after him; they've been doing this since the 1960s when they were teenagers themselves. I'll call you each week to let you know how it's going and what he's been up to," Leonie added.

By the time she left my parent's house, my mum was so reassured that she'd have driven me to the airport then and there if I'd asked.

In the weeks and months that followed, Leonie kept her word. She rang my mum each week of the tour, and if my parents ever needed to reach me, they could, as she'd be speaking to her husband (Lek) with whom I was touring.

It sounds so abstract even to have to remind you but remember, there were no mobile phones in 1988 and no Internet. We stayed in contact the old-fashioned way, passing messages on through intermediates and scheduling calls on landlines when we knew when and where we'd be by our tour schedule.

What Leonie didn't mention, because it hadn't happened yet, was that for the first time, I'd experience women throwing themselves at me. I'd get arrested in Dallas, end up as the band's bass player for three gigs and generally have an out-of-world experience. And do a gig with The Beach Boys.

I was to be away for three months and miss a bit of the college term (semester). My tutor told me to go. He'd have carried me to the airport; such was his belief that I'd learn far more on this tour in 12 weeks than sitting in a class.

Landing in New York City for the first time was magical, and getting the airport bus to the city and taking in things I'd only ever seen on TV was surreal. The first step on my long journey to Providence was The Port Authority bus station.

Fuck me. It was grim. The fairy tale ended abruptly on arrival when I got approached by multiple weirdos who wanted to:

1. Help me with my bags (steal them).
2. Give me directions (send me somewhere I'd be mugged).
3. Sell me something to make me happy beyond my wildest dreams (nothing legal).
4. Do something indescribable to my person (no thanks, I'm British!)

I had to push my way through this barrage of despots, ensuring the kung-fu grip on my luggage never slacked off to get to the ticket office window.

"Yeeeaaaaaah?" said the ticket agent with a wilful carelessness that bordered on disdain.

"Errr... single Greyhound to Providence, please," I said, but it must've seemed like I whispered it because...

"WHAT WAS THAT, MISTER?" She growled back at me. "TICKET-TO-PROVIDENCE-PLEASE!" I fired off quickly.

"The bus leaves from over there," she said, pointing at the stop as she **threw** my ticket at me.

Welcome to New York Port Authority, English boy!

With my ticket in hand, I shuffled my way to the bus stop, with more despots walking towards me like a zombie apocalypse. I kept my head down, my long hair over my face, and prayed the Greyhound bus would show up sooner rather than later.

Why I thought the Greyhound would be a safe refuge, lord knows. My first jet lag experience involved sitting next to a guy who was passionate about telling me all the things he loved about his pet snake.

The only problem was that his pet snake was in a box on his knee! Three hours and 40 minutes of bum-clench later, I arrived at the motel in Providence, Rhode Island. I was exhausted but pleased to see the promise of privacy, hygiene, and a snake-free bed.

Good morning USA!

The gig was an outdoor afternoon show at a local county fair. I'd get very acquainted with local and State Fairs in the States over the years as this was a staple of the touring schedule for a heritage band.

The first thing I had to do was speak to the promoter on the phone and run through the checklist. In a change to the European gigs, it was now my job to call ahead and do all the pre-gig checks. I was responsible for making everything happen. One of the challenges on a tour like this is that apart from guitars, you don't carry any equipment; it's all hired in by the promoter.

If the band members were lucky, then they'd get what they'd asked for. If they *weren't* lucky, then I had to sort it out. You can guess that, more often than not, there was work for me to do here.

For my first gig on this tour, the promoter was less than helpful on the phone, and when I got to the fair, it became apparent that I was the only person who would make *anything* happen.

All the kit was wrong, the stage crew and sound crew had no idea what the band's requirements were, and it all had to be fixed before the band arrived two hours later for sound check.

So, the nice English boy made friends with everyone and offered to do way more work than he should for the others in exchange for one thing. Decent equipment.

I somehow managed to convince the sound company to return to their warehouse, bring a genuine kit, and invoice the promoter. I'd do the rest.

I set the stage, and the merchandise table, briefed the various crews, and then the band arrived. It was great to see them, and the feeling was mutual, but things were running late, so the back-slapping had to wait.

This was a golden opportunity for me to learn more than ever.

"Are you the band's sound engineer?" the crew asked.

"[cough] Er... yes," I replied, trying to sound convincing.

That was it. I'd become the band's front-of-house sound guy by accident. But I loved it.

To their credit, the band were OK with most things providing that the stage set-up was correct for them, their monitoring was good, and the T-shirt sales were prepped. Anything else was optional.

So, at soundcheck, I got my fingers on the mixing desk after the local guys had checked that everything was working. I got to do the best bit without all the manual labour!

Man, I fell in love with outdoor gigs from this moment and running the sound front house for an audience of thousands was a blast.

The gig came and went without any problems. I got a pretty good sound mix, and I made the band sound a bit more impactful as I wasn't scared of making the walls, floor, and the old dears dentures rattle and shake, even for a 1960s pop band.

The effect was dramatic. The drummer could feel his playing come back to him every time he 'gave it some'... he looked like he had a spark of electricity running through him. The guitars were a little edgier and up in the mix, which cut through nicely as Lek was a tidy player.

The band could *feel* the sound, and in turn, the audience *felt* the band. The sun was shining, and I had to get the dollars flowing.

I'd met some of the band's regular followers at soundcheck, and I got them to agree to help me on the merchandising table. The girls were blonde, friendly and willing (to sell T-shirts), so I set them free and watched the dollars come in.

But it was not just the girls' wholesome 'apple pie' demeanour that sold. At the table, some of the crowd were asking for a photo and an autograph from the band. Then, I had the 'aha' moment.

Free autographs sold T-shirts at $10 a pop. The sales before autographs and after were massively different, and from that day on, the 'business model' was based on access to the band, free photos and autographs being the 'hook', and then we went for the upsell with the T-shirts.

"We made how much?" Lek exclaimed with a joyous exuberance as he looked at piles of hard currency tied up in bundles of 10s and 20s on the desk. It was like a scene out of a movie where 'the deal' was going down... only I wasn't breaking any laws.

"If you do a meet-and-greet at the end of every show and announce it from the stage at the end of your set, we'll rake it in," I told the band.

In a similar phenomenon to the Turkey Run, crowds of

middle-aged people, full of burgers, candyfloss and lite beer, swarmed the merchandising area.

Some didn't even know who the band were, but that didn't even matter; they just got caught up in the moment.

After the show was done and dusted, and 'the count' was done on merchandising, I discovered the power of another phenomenon. The power of the English accent.

Just hanging out backstage, local people wanted to speak to me to hear my accent. It was like I had a superpower.

All I needed to do was say 'Hello, how are you?' and I'd have a group of people around me. I wasn't even in the band. If I was lucky, some 'girls' under 60 years old would be captivated by my subtle Manchester accent.

We had a ton of gigs ahead of us. Some were gigs that paid real money, some less so, but because they were 'pass-through' gigs. We played these sets because they were on the way to the real money gig; it kept the expenses under control and a (hotel) roof over our heads.

Journeys of hundreds of miles daily were standard, and patterns of 'travel' behaviour started to emerge. I developed a taste for the chilli and saltine crackers at *any* 76 Truck Stop I could find and 2% chocolate milk for the cooler in the custom Dodge Ram van we were driving ourselves in.

But on the longest drives, especially if it was my turn behind the wheel, Jolt Cola kicked my Pro Plus tablets into the long grass with its double caffeine. Jolt Cola saved my tired ass behind the wheel on more than one occasion.

KEY LESSONS IN
LIFE AND BUSINESS

THERE'S NO SUCH THING AS A
FAIRY TALE IN BUSINESS

The idea and concept of going to America for three months, trading in that terrible van for a Boeing 747, was nice whilst it lasted.

Still, the moment I arrived at Port Authority, the fairy tale was over, and the hard work and the challenges that we often face in work and life got thrown in my face.

The zombie apocalypse at the bus station and the need to fade into the background was hard for an 80s rock poodle. The fact I kept my sanity and my luggage was down to pure wit and determination; you have to expect the unexpected.

Business is managing challenges, whether a batch of faulty products, upset customers, or a man with a live snake on a bus.

THE POWER OF CONTEXT

Context, by definition, is the interrelated conditions in which something exists or occurs. It's a critical component to the positioning of, well, anything.

In an experiment for the Washington Post, celebrated classical violinist Joshua Bell performed in the D.C. Metro as a busker and barely made $150 as most of the commuters just walked on by. Those who did stop didn't recognise the person of significance before them.

Bell can usually charge in excess $100 for each seat in a concert hall setting!

As humans, we use context as a mental shortcut to quickly frame our understanding of something and, importantly, if we should even care about it.

By changing Bell's context, 'listeners' understood him to be something other than what he really is. Therefore, context matters.

In my case, in England, my accent was the same as everyone else's. The only difference was I looked like a hairy girl and worked with rock and roll/pop bands.

However, if you put me in upstate New York, Texas, Arkansas, Alabama, Kansas, Iowa, Wisconsin or, in this case, Rhode Island, I was something different. I was windswept and interesting, in demand, a curiosity to be investigated, and in some isolated incidents, I was desirable to women.

I wasn't used to the attention, but I can't say I didn't like it. I loved it and made every syllable I spoke count when needed. If circumstances at a gig required it, I'd bring out my best Queen's English accent.

By being in a different context, my positioning had changed, and wow, it had some power.

CHAPTER 8

WON'T GET FOOLED AGAIN

"**S**hek, Paul's dad just died," said Lek. We'd just finished a gig at a forgettable venue somewhere in Massachusetts. I had no clue anything was wrong.

"Shit, Paul, I'm so sorry, man," I said as I reached over and put my arm around him.

"Thanks, Shek. That's not all," Paul replied. "I'm flying back to Manchester tomorrow for a few days. I need you to take my place. We need you to be the new bass player!"

"Err... what the... but... I don't know how to play the songs, and I'm left-handed... I can't play your (right-handed) bass guitar."

Apparently, I could. And I did! Just like Jimi Hendrix did, only with (obviously) less earth-shattering talent.

The next show was the following night on Nantucket Island off the coast of Cape Cod. So, I had very little time to practise.

As we drove to Boston's Logan Airport to drop Paul off on our way to Cape Cod, I practised being Herman's Hermits' new bass player in the back of the van. Paul did everything he could to help. He had a cassette recording of that night's show on his Sony Walkman, had written the chord charts out for each song and restrung his bass guitar upside down so a lefty like me could play it.

Driving through the night, we sat in the back of the van, going through the set, song by song. I learnt the chords and backing vocals. Once we dropped Paul off at the airport, I had just 70 miles of road ahead to finish learning 90 minutes of live music.

I was absolutely crapping myself. The band were relying on me as there were a slew of shows coming up, and cancelling wasn't an option.

The first gig was in some beach club, and the first and only time I'd get to rehearse with the band was at the soundcheck.

Come showtime, the bum clench was getting tighter, as were my trousers. I was wearing Paul's stage clothes, but he was at least 1 foot shorter than me. This was far from comfortable.

I had the chord sheets laid out to my left, behind a stage apron so no one could see. They were my safety net. Before I knew it, Bean on drums counted us in, 1-2-3! And we were into the first song. In key, in time, and everything!

Who would know I wasn't even an original member? The fact that I was 19 and had very long hair might've been a give-away, but no one cared. I managed to get through two sets of 45 minutes without major musical incidents and kept clean underwear.

The relief afterwards was palpable. The gratitude from the band was measurable. I felt respect from the guys for what had (had to) happen.

The following two shows were at a Massachusetts State County fair, and I can only remember two things about it:

1. The stage was actually the back of a truck, I kid you not, and
2. Paul came back.

Halfway through the set on the second night, Paul walked on stage with his case straight off the flight from Boston in a long coat and old-fashioned flat cap. He stood next to me with a shit-eating grin as I played his gig.

The audience had no idea what was going on. They and the promoter thought a local had had too much to drink and decided to get on stage. I could see security guys approaching the stage, but just as the current song finished, Paul gave me a whopping kiss and strapped a bass guitar on.

Where on earth an additional (right-handed) bass guitar came from, Lord only knows.

I might've been the shortest-lived member of Herman's Hermits, but I was happy to get back to what I was supposed to be doing – running the business of the show.

Over the next few weeks, we played many shows in and around Wisconsin or Iowa, and we'd stay with friends of the band, Steve and Janice, who lived in Milwaukee. This was especially handy when there was downtime and no income, as it saved the tour budget.

Steve was originally a mega fan of the band back in the '60s, and what he didn't know about 60s music wasn't worth knowing. He had wardrobes of original vinyl records from the era. His mental recall of 60s music and vast record collection was computer-like.

We killed our time mooching around pawn shops for old guitars and musical curiosities, barbecuing, and forging relationships. I also spent quite a bit of time with original members Lek and Barry (aka 'Bean'). They talked frankly about the old days; what they had experienced was *incredible*. They'd rubbed shoulders with Elvis and The Beatles, appeared on the Ed Sullivan Show, and played at the biggest stadiums in America.

One of their stories stuck out from the rest. A story that is widely acknowledged as one of *the* rock and roll stories of all time. And I was getting the story from the source, guys who were actually there...

In 1967, Herman's Hermits were a huge deal in America.

The Monterey International Pop Festival ran from June 16th–18th, 1967, in Northern California, attracting 200,000 people over three days. An event that introduced US audiences to Jimi Hendrix, Janis Joplin, and Otis Redding, to name but three.

And Herman's Hermits were doing a headline tour of America at the height of their popularity.

And their support band? An 'up-and-coming' band from London who were doing their first North American tour called The Who.

Yes, *The Who.*

The Who have arguably been called the godfathers of hard rock. Their performance of "My Generation" on prime-time TV provided an explosive introduction to American prime-time audiences.

And Keith Moon was their renowned 'wild' drummer. Not one for holding back, Moon's style was considered the inspiration for the character 'Animal' from The Muppets, and he lived his life as he played his drums. Without compromise. On the edge.

After the gig in question in Flint, Michigan, the band and their entourage returned to the Holiday Inn in a celebratory mood. It was Keith's 21st birthday, and plenty of 'guests' were drawn towards the hotel's swimming pool, which faced the car park. They jumped in, fully clothed.

And from thereon in, the party *really* got going. Exploding toilets and fire extinguishers set off were prequels to the 5-rise drum-shaped cake that the Premier Drum company had sent to the party. Complete with a girl jumping out of it. Of course.

Happy Birthday, Keith! Jeez, I wish I'd been there too!

Keith seemed to think throwing the cake at the party guests would be a great idea, and a food fight ensued in the hotel lobby. Icing and marzipan everywhere! Keith got increasingly naked as time passed, and inevitably, the cops arrived at the height of the festivities.

The birthday boy disappeared and jumped into a Lincoln Continental town car, releasing the handbrake. He didn't consider that the car was on a slight incline, and the car rolled backwards through the fence and into the deep end of the swimming pool! With Keith Moon still inside it!

Despite Keith spending time in county jail, causing $24,000 of damage (equivalent to $195,000 in today's money), he some-how made The Who's next tour stop in Philadelphia, courtesy of a chartered plane.

Following the incident, the band were banned for life from staying at Holiday Inn hotels, anywhere, until the ban was lifted in 1999. 32 years later.

I'm sure that Keith had years of countless other incidents. Tragically, his renowned hedonism caught up with him, and he died on 7th September 1978, from a massive accidental drug overdose.

During our time at Steve and Janice's home, I also learnt more about the band's struggles from the early days to the present, focusing on two areas. Their former lead singer and money.

Their original lead singer, Peter Noone, left the band in 1971, and there wasn't much of a relationship afterwards. When I say relationship, there *really* wasn't one, nor were there many respectful references about him. At best, he was referred to as 'Noone'... after a few beers, the names got more creative and somewhat savoury!

Peter Noone was the band's focal point in the 1960s, so much so that in the early days, people thought he *was* 'Herman' and the Hermits were just his backing band. This clearly grated on the rest of the band as they, Lek especially, were accomplished musicians and an equal part of the band. But perception is reality, and this was something that existed, so much so that even in 1988, over 20 years after the band's peak, people asked me, "Hey, where's Herman?"

The other issue relating to the band's former lead singer was more common to popular bands after their heyday, especially when they went their separate ways. Who owns the name of the band?

If the remaining band members want to keep playing professionally and use the name, somebody must agree. The name, after all, is an intangible asset you can make money from.

The argument went like this. The band's main members claimed the name Herman's Hermits should stay with them as they were still active, and the majority of the original members were still playing in the band. Peter Noone argued that he was the focal point of the band as the original lead singer. Thus, people associate him with the name Herman's Hermits. After all, he *was* Herman.

During my time with the band, the agreement on the name was that they could use the name Herman's Hermits as they'd never stopped touring (ever!), and there were still two original band members in the line-up. Peter Noone was simply billed as Peter Noone of Herman's Hermits.

However, these things are fluid. Since the sad passing of Derek Leckenby, Herman's Hermits now only have one original member. They still tour, 60 years on, as Herman's Hermits, but now they can no longer tour in America. Why the change in America?

The USA is Peter Noone's backyard and with only one original member left from the main band, Barry Whitwam, that in soccer terms is a score draw, one original member a piece!

Aside from the difficulties with Peter Noone, I saw a bigger problem with the other elephant on the tour bus. Money.

I often heard Lek and Bean talking about what was owed by whom. Even in the late 80s and early 90s, when I worked for them, they'd go to New York to see their lawyers over this issue. Sure, I heard plenty of heated discussions and felt their angst over this.

Like many early pop-era musicians, the Hermits were railroaded by the industry and mismanaged. As chronicled in the book 'Baby, You're a Rich Man: Suing the Beatles for Fun & Profit', the band fought for years to gain its due royalties.

In September 1965, the group's Hermusic sued producers and handlers Mickie Most and Allen Klein. It wasn't until February 2013 that the Hermits (via their publishing entity Chimeron LLC) were awarded overdue royalties in court.

Lek tragically passed away of non-Hodgkin's lymphoma in 1994, aged just 51. I toured with him in the States whilst he was having treatment after his diagnosis. It still distresses me greatly that he never learnt that after what must have seemed a lifetime of fighting, the Hermits won their case in court.

When he died, he was younger than I am now. I still fucking miss him. Shit, I'm crying writing this.

KEY LESSONS IN LIFE AND BUSINESS

EXPECT THE UNEXPECTED

Sometimes life throws you a curve ball. I never expected that I'd have to step into Paul's shoes when his dad died. But I managed to do it because I was so determined to do it. The band had faith in me too.

I've had a boss who's been my boss twice in two different companies. But he used to have a boss who gave him a great piece of advice that he shared with me. He always used to say, "At any moment, we can all get fired."

When we worked together in one company, it was particularly volatile. I must've almost gotten fired three times through no fault of my own, but I probably never knew it. Even though we don't work together still, we have a close relationship. He always says to be prepared for what's next. Whatever that is, it's not a threat. Always have something ready to go.

The experience of playing with the band was probably the first experience I had of being ready for what was next, and I wasn't really prepared. But I had the personal tools, aptitude, and desire to make it work.

HELP YOUR COLLEAGUES WHEN THEY NEED HELP

This was also about being able to help someone else when it mattered. It wasn't life or death, but the band had three gigs coming up that they couldn't cancel. It was their livelihood. You need to be willing to help your colleagues when they need the help, even if it forces you out of your comfort zone.

It might not be so directly important to you but recognise when it's important to significant others. And it helps you put equity in the bank of the people you work with. One day, you'll need to draw down on it, so pull it off no matter how difficult it may be. It'll be remembered forever.

There's a difference between people who can and people who can't. Help your friends and family when you have the opportunity; they won't forget it. Be the person they can turn to when they're facing challenges.

TAKE CARE OF BUSINESS

To accuse most legacy bands of failure to take care of business, would be incredibly harsh on them. They were minnows swimming in a sea of sharks.

The music industry has come a long way but even judging from my recent side hustles, working with major labels and publishers still requires you to have your business wits about you and a focus on detail.

Even in our day jobs, attention to detail can make or break us. Think about some oversized ticket items and the consequences of not getting it right. Or negotiating salary and terms for a new job.

Setting out objectives and key results as a source of measurement, are we setting ourselves up for success? Or inevitable failure?

CHAPTER 9

THE SHOW MUST GO ON

"**W**ow, that sounded incredible, well done lads," I said, giving Lek and Rod a thumbs up from behind the studio console.

We were on break from the tour and had some free studio time in Milwaukee. It was great to see the band in full swing, trying new material after all these years.

"Can we just try it again from the chorus and try to rock it up a bit," I added, knowing the band would be desperate to nip outside for a fag. But I couldn't resist as we were so close to perfection.

I was behind the large studio mixing desk and loved it. I was back creating, and it was magic. I'd learned the ropes in three days from Daryll, the studio's first engineer.

Frank, the studio's owner, came into the room. He was more like a friendly Mafiosi, your lively neighbourhood wise guy. For all I knew, he was, but he was good to me and people he considered his friends.

"Harvey, how do you fancy moving to America and coming to work for me here in the studio? Daryll's leaving in two months, and I'm going to be a man down," Frank proposed.

"What? Really?" 19 year old me sputtered.

"Let's not dress it up for more than it is. I can't get you a green card, pay you much, and you'll sleep on the couch in the studio control room. But I need a new first engineer soon, and I like you; you've got the chops for it. Whaddya say?" he said.

I loved America. And America threw her arms open and made it clear I was more than welcome.

"That's a brilliant offer; thank you so much. I love the idea of me working here," I replied. "Can I think about it? It's a big change, a lot to mull over."

"Sure, that's fine, but you'll have to let me know by the end of the week," he said as he left the room.

My mind was awash with possibilities. Whom would I meet? The skills and experience I'd gain would firmly put me on a career path in recording music. I even liked Milwaukee! Maybe I'd marry an American and have some wholesome apple-pie kids.

In the car with the band's friend Stephen, I talked it through, and like any good friend, he gave me a strong dose of reality.

"Let's go and see what a car here will cost you," he suggested. "You can't live in America without a car."

So off to a local dealer we went.

"What do you think you can afford?" he prodded.

"What do I need?" I innocently asked.

"You likely won't get anything that'll actually drive for less than $5,000."

Bang! That was like a kick in the teeth, "I've not got that kind of money," I replied. "I might be able to scrape it together if I ask my mum and dad."

Before I spoke to them, I wanted to see what $5,000 would get me. The sales guy had one. Just one. And what a fucking rust bucket.

It was a royal blue estate car with wood panelling down the

side and blue velour seats that had the smell of a sinister history about them. Has someone been killed in this car? Were Xenomorphs living in it? I was looking for evidence of blood or alien slime. Really, it was *so* bad.

When we started the engine, it sounded like a bag of large spanners being shaken violently. And the sound did not get better when we took it for a spin.

"What do you think, kid?" the salesman questioned whilst gently rubbing his hands in glee.

I couldn't buy the car. Even in the excitement of the idea of moving to America, the reality of the matter was that I would be an illegal alien, have no definitive salary and not even be able to sleep in a real bed. Never mind the car!

I couldn't do it. After some reflection, the practicalities of it outweighed the promise of it.

The following day, I made my way back to the studio, a little crestfallen but glad that I was going with my head and not just my heart.

Twenty minutes later, I got caught in the crossfire of the band talking about some of their original recordings. I'd had no idea that half of Led Zeppelin had played on many of their songs – Herman's Hermits were heavier than I thought.

It turns out that Jimmy Page was a busy session player before shredding his way to the status of a hard rock idol. The guitarist played the guitar on everything from girl group records to folk cuts. Page and his future Led Zep bassist, John Paul Jones, were studio players on many Hermits hits. Jimmy [Page] played on 'Silhouettes' and 'Wonderful World' and, once [Hermits' bassist] Karl Green faded, he was replaced on *all* of the recordings by John Paul Jones.

After listening to the band talk, I realised I needed to learn more from them. A move to America might've been off for me, but there was still much of the tour ahead.

We left the following Friday for a package bill in Iowa, and I never returned to that little studio in Milwaukee.

So, what was the package bill? Promoters often packaged up multiple bands from a particular era to help add appeal to a show, especially if the venue was large. No single band on these kinds of shows could sell 5,000-10,000 tickets alone. But if you group five or six well-known legacy bands, you have a very different proposition. All of a sudden, it's a broader trip down memory lane. It's packageable and marketable.

We were destined for big venues in Des Moines, Cedar Rapids and Dubuque, joining up with The Byrds, who were headlining, with Herman's Hermits being second on the bill.

It only took about two minutes of being in Des Moines, the location of the first show, for the shit to hit the fan. We got to the hotel, and all the bands and crew were sitting in the lobby.

Lek turned to a massive guy with large tattoos and arms the size of tree trunks to find out what was happening.

"I don't believe it! What are we going to do?" Bean started pacing the floor.

"Shekel, we're in deep shit. The promoter had gone bankrupt before the shows even started," Lek added.

What a mess. It was the day of the first show, and someone in charge had some big decisions to make. The problem was that there was no one. The promoter had done a runner, leaving an almighty mess behind.

The reality of the matter was that there was no money. No one would get paid, and to add insult to injury, all of the artists would be out of pocket for their tour expenses.

So, after 30 minutes or so of collective disbelief, everyone agreed to have one key band member represent their respective band at a crunch meeting in the hotel lobby. Lek, as the band leader, stepped forward as he often did.

The decision was to carry on and do all three shows, providing the sound and lighting companies, venues and crews agreed. If anyone vetoed, the whole thing would be off. And after some frantic phone calls, the shows were ON!

However, there was another problem: they needed a person to help make things happen from a production point of view.

"I'll do it...," I volunteered, stepping forward into this unknown upside-down world.

I ended up working for six bands and near-single-handedly got the production done. The show was a huge success.

My lasting memory of the night was striking up a rapport with Jon Bauman in the hotel's bar. I knew what he had done in his career, but that night was memorable because he took the time and, with such sincerity, gave me his respect for what I had done for the show's good. Not only this, he openly championed me to the other bands and crew. He didn't have to do that.

You may not know who Jon 'Bowzer' Bauman is. He's best known for being a part of the band Sha Na Na during the 70s, and I remember him as the only person I've ever met who featured in the 1978 film, *Grease*, one of my favourite films!

Sha Na Na, featured in the film as 'Johnny Casino and the Gamblers' and 'Bowzer', can clearly be seen in the movie strutting his stuff to 'Hound Dog'. To this day, I'm kicking myself for not remembering any of the John Travolta or Olivia Newton-John stories he told me.

For the following two shows, we decided to give *all* the tickets away for free via local radio stations so we'd have full stadiums to play to (and to maximise our T-shirt sales).

Then we headed east towards New England for three consecutive shows. Whoever put the itinerary together was mad. The first show was in Boston (on the East Coast), followed by the second show in Hollywood (on the West Coast) and finally, Milwaukee (in the Midwest). We had three shows to do and 4,740 miles to cover in less than 48 hours.

The logistics went like this.

After the Boston show, I had to drop the band off at Logan Airport so they could fly to LA to do the show the next day. I then had to drive from Boston, with my non-negotiable target being to pick the band up 36 hours later from the airport in Chicago and then drive them to Milwaukee to do the show.

It was a game of drive-fly-drive leapfrog. And for me, a near 1,000-mile drive by myself with a drive-by in Chicago to pick up the band and then play a show, 92 miles up the I-94 same night in Milwaukee.

Man, that drive was long, and I practically had to drive non-stop to be confident I'd get to the airport to pick up the band from their flight back from LA. In one stretch, I made it to South Bend, Illinois, to a motel for four hours of sleep. With a few stops, it was 18 hours of driving, but it got me very close to Chicago, meaning the next day, I'd have all the pressure off, and it'd be more 'normal'.

Wrong!

I headed to O'Hare airport to pick the band up late afternoon as planned. But something wasn't quite right. The first sign, the band did not show up within an hour of their flight landing. I drove around and around the pick-up zones but nada. I paid to park and went into arrivals. Why was their flight not showing? I simply didn't understand. Did I have the wrong day? Was I a day early? Not according to the tour itinerary.

So, I found a payphone, put my quarter in and called the band's manager, Julie, in LA.

"Shekel, where the hell are you?" she barked down the phone.

"I'm at the airport as planned!" I stated.

"Hold on, I've got Lek on the other line, very irate. He says he and the band are at the airport too. I'm going to put the two handsets together so you can talk to each other directly," she said.

"Shek, where the fuck are you? We landed two hours ago!" Lek shrieked down the phone.

"I'm at the airport, Lek, as planned." I was baffled.

"Which airport?" Lek questioned.

'O'Hare, of course," I replied confidently.

"Fuck! We are at Midway Airport across town! Hold on..."

I'd gone to the wrong airport, hadn't I? The itinerary stated 'Chicago Airport', but I had no idea there were two airports in Chicago! After a right royal kerfuffle down the phone, Lek came back on.

"Right, fucking stay there, we're coming to you. I've hired a limo, we'll be about 30 minutes," Lek said forcefully.

None of this would have been much of an issue on any typical day. But we had a show the same day, and we'd burnt hours with this mess, and in all honesty, I had no idea if we'd make the show in Milwaukee.

How I'd have loved a mobile phone in 1988!

The band eventually pulled up in a black Lincoln stretch town car like it was a scene out of the Blues Brothers movie. They bundled into our Dodge van, and I slammed my foot to the floor, leaving any trace of restraint firmly behind us.

Any talk of what had happened was put on hold as we focused on trying to get to the show in Milwaukee. By our calculations, we'd get there 30 mins before showtime. We'd been supposed to be there four hours earlier for the soundcheck, but there was no way.

We arrived just 15 minutes before showtime. A huge audience of thousands waiting and a promoter who, by all appearances, was having a heart attack in the street.

I did a quick sweep of the kit on the stage, barked some orders to the local crew, and the band walked up onto the stage with one minute to spare. I ran to the front of the house and jumped on the sound mixing desk. Breathe, Harvey, breathe!

1-2-3, and we were off. I did a few tweaks and fades here and there, and the sound came together really quickly. It ended up being a great show, but boy, it had been the most stressful day of my life. I would never assume anything ever again.

KEY LESSONS IN
LIFE AND BUSINESS

MAKE SURE YOUR WORK IS MEANINGFUL TO YOU

I could've taken things easy during the free studio time, gone shopping, or dicked around. But I deputised for the studio's engineer when I got the chance and tried to learn as much as possible from him. If you make sure your work is meaningful, you'll be motivated, it'll likely create opportunities, and you'll get noticed. Maybe not immediately, but if you're consistent, the universe will look after you.

KNOW WHEN TO SAY NO

Not taking the job the studio boss offered me was the first time I said no to something substantial that I cared about. It seemed like a dream opportunity, but the reality was too harsh. I wasn't prepared to drop out of college to do it, be destitute or drive a wreck.

I've learned over the years that it's hard to say no to things you feel torn about. As Professor Scott Galloway says in his book 'The Algebra of Happiness', "Nothing is ever as good or as bad as it seems."

You have to do some soul searching, look deeply into the situation, and try to play out future scenarios of how it might work out, best-case and worst-case scenarios.

Learning to say no is an essential skill. And actually, learning *how* to break the news to people is important too.

DON'T EVER MAKE ASSUMPTIONS

I naively assumed that the band was flying into the one-and-only airport I knew in Chicago. That was wrong.

In business, often, things aren't completely as they seem. Interpretation or the source of the data, the reputation of a particular individual, or the optics in a leadership team meeting. There are always at least two dimensions to everything, sometimes three.

Over the years, I've become incredibly detail-oriented, sometimes to the point of splitting hairs to get to the truth. I often hear private clients say, 'we assume that' or 'our assumption was'. At this point, I know I have work to do to validate it or bust the myth in which they believe.

CHAPTER 10

ROUTE 66

"**G**entlemen," said the HUGE cop outside the venue after the Dallas show.

"Who's responsible for selling the merchandise?" he questioned.

We all looked at each other, slightly puzzled.

"Erm. I am," I said.

"Can I see your permit please?" he growled.

"Permit? What permit? The venue or promoter didn't advise us we needed a permit," I politely defied.

Out came the handcuffs. Jeez. As I was getting my rights read, I was getting frogmarched into the black and white police car. What the hell was happening? The band turned their backs and got in the tour van. Thanks a bunch, fellas!

Just as my head was being guided down into the back seat, the band walked over to say their goodbyes. They stood there looking at me in the cop car as if to say, 'we knew he was a bad penny.'

But then I caught Bean's sly grin out of the corner of my eye. It was a fucking setup! Bean knew I'd clocked him; he was never very good at a poker face! He was the least serious person I knew, and he was more than twice my age!

Everyone started pissing themselves with laughter, even the cop. He was an old friend of the band and had been game for stitching me up. I didn't admit it, but that single minute in the back of a police car 4,600 miles from home had felt like a lifetime.

We played some great gigs in Arkansas, Texas, and Arizona and did a residency in Las Vegas.

The Texas gig was the most exciting and engaging. I loved the attitude of the Texans, and the welcome was pure Texas and cowboy boots. How could I not love it? The hotel was called the Harvey Hotel!

I remember Phoenix as the hottest, driest place I've ever been to (until I spent much time in the Middle East years later!). It's also home to the hottest buffalo wings to ever grace my stomach. The gig was OK but playing a set in between a line-dancing session is certainly different! 'Yee-Haw' meets 'How Do You Do?' is the musical equivalent of oil and water.

Our route to Vegas saw us deliberately join up to the famous Route 66. We were stopping off in Flagstaff, Arizona, in saloons, enjoying the purposeful touristic artefacts along the way. A detour to the Grand Canyon with incredible views was nothing compared to the nauseous bum-clenching experience of driving over Hoover Dam.

But despite the new touristic aspect to our schedule, the long drives and lighter schedule provided a time for reflection. I was whiling away the miles and the hours, gazing out the window. Thinking. I was just thinking.

What would I do when I got home? Would I go back to music college? I had always assumed so, but I was starting to feel differently.

But first, Las Vegas.

Nevada would be one of the States I'd spend quite a bit of time in over the upcoming years, as the band always seemed to get a residency in a casino town. Lake Tahoe, Reno or Vegas. I spent weeks at a time there, and the worst thing about it was the sheer boredom!

In the desert for weeks, days to kill, you'd blow all your money on keeping yourself occupied.

Despite the little things like getting mistaken for being David Coverdale (of Whitesnake) in Macy's, shooting guns on a range or being aghast at Nazi memorabilia in a pawn shop, the longer you were there, the more desperate for entertainment you became.

Our self-enforced rule of no daytime drinking was the only thing that saved us from getting very messy come showtime.

Fortunately, the evenings were entertaining. The place came alive, and memories of topless showgirls and occasional loose (*slightly* drunk) women mesmerised by an English accent are still ingrained in the memory. I still can't figure out why, when I stood at the side of the stage watching 20-or-so topless girls do their thing, they 'covered up' when they came off. Hundreds of people had just seen almost everything there was to be seen (to music), and there were only a handful of us backstage.

A production manager made it very clear to me before the first Vegas show that there was **no fraternising with the showgirls.** Or else. 'Tis with a heavy heart I have to tell you that despite being surrounded by beautiful topless showgirls, semi-dressed in feathers, I was hardly even allowed to look.

What a miss. Even for a David Coverdale look-alike!

During my three weeks in residency at the Four Queens Hotel in Vegas, I had more time to reflect than I bargained for. The tour would soon be ending.

A gig at UCLA in California and a headline set at the New York State Fair brought the 89-day tour to an end.

Incredible memories for a now 20-year-old with aspirations in music. I'd done three shows with the Beach Boys (did they really need *four* tour buses?), ridden the elevator with Frankie Valli, and met and socialised with Flo and Eddie from The Turtles.

And so, we returned to the airport in Chicago, the correct airport this time! It was time to go back to Manchester, England. It was time to go back to music college.

Or was it?

KEY LESSONS IN LIFE AND BUSINESS

TAKE THE TIME TO THINK

"The most important thinking is thinking about thinking," cite the kings of category creation, The Category Pirates, in their book, "Snow Leopard".

In 2018, Professor Mark Ritson wrote about George Shultz, President Ronald Reagan's secretary of state. He said that each week he would scrupulously seek out solitude for one hour. He explained that he would leave specific instructions that only the President or his wife were allowed to disturb him. And with the door closed behind him, he would engage in that most unusual of activities – he'd think.

In business, we're all too quick to act, to do *something*, and to make a difference by doing. Tactics and go-to-market take precedence over everything. Often at the unfortunate expense of not thinking about what we *are* doing.

But tactics, the execution of your plan, is just that. It's the tactification of strategy. And strategy is about choice, and as Harvard Professor Michael Porter puts it, "Strategy is choosing what *not* to do."

HERMAN'S HERMITS

◀ 1988 Nantucket Island, MA. The relief was palpable after my first gig as Herman's Hermit's shortest-serving band member. My unplanned stint was three gigs I'll never forget.

More limos! This time with Derek 'Lek' Leckenby (RIP) and his wife, Leonie, on our way to a Herman's Hermit's gig in Hollywood, CA, in the 80s. ▼

◄ Reno, NV. My big hair and English accent caused someone to mistake me for David Coverdale of Whitesnake later that day.

▲ Following a show in America in 1992. Nobody could have predicted that a decade later, I would become an employee of Microsoft - least of all myself.

CHAPTER 11

LEAP OF FAITH

"**H**arvey, will you do me a favour and hang out the washing when the washer beeps?" asked my Mum.

"And if you could tidy away all your guitars before dinner, that'd be great," my Dad added.

Arriving back in Britain had been more of a metaphoric personal crash-landing than a homecoming. It was an utterly deflating experience.

My time in the States had helped me see 'possibilities' beyond my previous understanding of the world, and I wanted to explore and take them. But now I was back home with my parents, and it felt like there was no way out.

Life got dull very quickly.

I went back to music college as planned, but my perspective differed. Before the tour, college was my opportunity, my growth. Coming back, I saw the students in a very narrow light. What I had experienced, my fellow students never would. No longer did I see college as the solution to what I wanted to do. This was a problem.

My education wasn't taking up all my time; I needed more after being busy non-stop for three months. Much more.

I decided to take on some work from the concert sound company temporarily. I did my £5 and bag-of-chips job. I became their second engineer for casual local and UK-wide work.

Most of the gigs were weekend work and around Manchester or the North West of England, so I could do it around college.

Battle-of-the-bands, the 60s, 70s, and even some more recent 80s bands all became the staple of the work. But one booking stood out and became a complete life changer for me.

"Harvey, can you do a gig tomorrow?" my boss Geoff said.

"Erm, sure, yes," I replied, thinking it was local as usual.

"It's in Sunderland; we must be there by lunchtime for sound checks. It's a battle of the bands. I'll accept the booking then," he quickly said before putting the phone down. I had no time to backtrack.

It was a four to five-hour drive each way with six bands in between. It was going to be a long day and night.

The city of Sunderland, in the North East of England, was a former shipbuilding and coal mining heartland. Proud people found that as the world changed around them, everything they and generations of their families had known had dissolved away.

One thing the good people of Sunderland still had was a wicked, cutting sense of humour and the ability to have a great night out. Beers, music and 'the crack' are central to this. *Crack* is a term for news, gossip, fun, entertainment, and enjoyable conversation, particularly prominent in Ireland, where it's known as *craic. In short, it's about having a laugh.*

Two notable things happened that day:

1. I had the hottest curry of my life (don't ask me how I remember it was a Sri Lankan chicken takeaway over 30 years after the fact!)
2. I witnessed the best local unsigned band I'd *ever* seen.

The Troubleshooters were a 4-piece melodic rock band with a classic formula in their line-up. Featuring two brothers, a good-looking lead singer and a highly energetic and accomplished lead guitarist, backed by a really solid rhythm section.

Chris (vocals) had the thing that any lead singer should have, apart from all the girls wanting him. A fantastic distinctive voice. When *he* sang, *you* knew who it was.

Baz (guitar) was rock guitar's equivalent of the Energizer Bunny! He *never* stopped moving. How he played without dropping a note was a wonder of the world. At one point, he was in the crowd stomping on the tables as he soloed. Bewildered audience members looked puzzled and delighted at the same time as Baz practically impaled them on his Fender Telecaster.

It was by far the best set of songs and performances of the night. They *had* to be clear winners.

They lost.

It was a complete travesty; the band's own sense of injustice was evident. I made my way over to see them just before the (kit) tear-down and *heavily* empathised.

You might ask why they were so distraught. It was just a gig and £100 prize money, after all. But they were *very serious* about making their band work professionally. A win would've given them enough to pay for some studio time, and they'd have been able to cut a demo tape.

Earlier in the day (pre-curry), I'd been chatting to Baz, and it turned out that he was no stranger to being in a band at a much higher level. As a bass player, Baz had been in a Sunderland band called the Toy Dolls, known in the UK for the chart hit 'Nelly the Elephant'.

Baz joined the Toy Dolls in 1983, and recorded two singles but left the band just before they had a smash hit single with a re-recorded version of 'Nelly the Elephant'. It sold 535,000 copies and peaked at number 4 on the charts.

He formed the Troubleshooters in 1985, three years before I met him with a keen eye for success. So, it's understandable that the angst I saw at not winning was three years or more of frustration coming to the fore.

The band spoke of needing help, a manager or someone who could help elevate them out of being 'just' another local unsigned band. I was enthused and empathised, gave them my (parents') phone number, and I went back home to Manchester.

A few months later, I returned from college one day, and my mum had a message for me. Baz had phoned.

I rang him back.

"Aaaaallreeeeeeeeet 'Arv man?!" Baz greeted me down the phone in a way only he could.

We chatted about what was going on with the band, and he invited me back to Sunderland to see them play a gig that weekend. I agreed straight away. I didn't expect much, but it beat being at home and being asked to do chores.

I arrived in Sunderland at 7pm on the Friday. After all the pleasantries of seeing each other again, a gig was to be done. The band were playing at Sinatra's bar that night, and fuck me, it was packed. Hundreds of people squashed in like tinned sardines, sweat dropping from the ceiling. The band did their thing and took the roof off with a raucous set.

I couldn't understand how an unknown band with their talent could stay this unknown. Word did get out, as it happens, but it didn't travel further than 5-10 miles in any direction. The A&R guys from the London record labels were hardly beating a path to hang out on the streets of Sunderland. Manchester, maybe with its famous vibrant music scene, but not Sunderland.

The conversation the next day, ironically sitting in Sinatra's bar, turned unexpectedly from jovial crack to business.

I had recently concluded that touring in any capacity or being a studio engineer was OK, but not truly what I wanted to do.

I liked the deal-making, the money and the contract side. I wanted my future to be around managing the business of music, not recording it.

The Troubleshooters wanted and needed someone to help them spread their wings and reach their goal. They wanted to get a recording contract and go professional. I knew in my heart of hearts that I needed to break out of what I was doing if I wanted to develop further.

The lads (and Baz especially) made a direct proposal.

"Manage us, Harvey. You know it makes sense!" Baz proposed succinctly.

Actually, on paper, it made *no sense*. I had a college course to complete and some sort of future ahead of me. But without too much thought, I went with my heart.

I agreed to manage the band and relocate to Sunderland.

It took all of five minutes to arrange and for me to agree to be roommates with the manager of Sinatra's bar – even though I'd only just met him and I'd not seen his flat.

As I made my way home to Manchester on the National Express bus (the British equivalent to a Greyhound bus), I realised I had two weeks to convince my parents and move my life 141 miles north to Sunderland. What the fuck was I thinking?

As soon as I got back, I ripped the plaster off and broke the news to my poor, bewildered parents. Despite all the logic and well-reasoned arguments about why I should *not* go, I stood defiant that I was going, even though it still made no logical sense.

It took a lot to leave the music course I'd worked so hard to get on, but I felt destiny was calling me, and I had to say *adios*. A one-way van ride later, I'd left home at age 20 without money, and reality soon hit me in the face.

If anything personified the life I was about to lead, it was the flat I was to share with Paul. The top floor of a run-down four-storey townhouse would've been magnificent in its heyday. My bedroom was big enough for the bed, which had no legs and sat on cinder block bricks.

The flat was grim but cheap. I had a 14" black and white TV with a loop aerial and dial to 'tune in'. I couldn't cook, I feared I'd catch something from the bathroom as the hygiene was that poor, and my newfound flatmate, Paul, was an alcoholic. Hardly an original problem, given he managed a bar.

My lasting memory of Paul was that he came back late each night drunk as a skunk. And that one night, at about 1am, he came back rat-arse drunk with two girls. One for him and...

"Here you go, Harvey, I brought this one for you," he said as he barged into my cinder-block bedroom and woke me up. He parked her friend on the corner of my bed whilst he stumbled to his room with her friend to try to get it on.

All I could do was apologise, make the poor lass a cup of tea and keep her company whilst we listened awkwardly to her friend next door go through some drunken horror movie routine. The screaming was horrendous, but the only unifying point we could find was that neither of us knew if it was Paul or her friend.

Maybe it was no surprise that just a few weeks later, Paul got fired from his job and left the flat. It was then up to me to manage 100% of the costs.

Once I had gotten used to my new reality, it was time to focus on why I was there.

Being the best-known band in Sunderland was going to get us nowhere. It was clear the Troubleshooters had to be the biggest band in the whole of the North East or even the whole of the North of England, and they had to break through and raise their profile in London.

But making that happen was the hard part. This was 1989, and the Internet as we know it didn't exist. Social proof was the old-fashioned word of mouth and a few kind words from a reporter in the local newspaper.

National radio only consisted of one station that mattered. There were few-to-no outlets for the band's music, let alone a band without a record label.

So, the strategy chose itself. We had to approach it the old-fashioned but tried-and-tested way. Hard graft on the road, take the music (and the show) to the people and gig like there was no tomorrow.

Fortunately, the band lived for playing shows, this was their forte and the environment I discovered them in. So, I hit the phone and rang every pub, bar and club in North East England to convince them to book the band. Hundreds of demo tapes and one-pagers got sent out. The day's CRM and project management tool was handwritten entries into a hardback A4 day-a-page view diary.

The gigs came in and continued to come in. Referrals, word of mouth, and relentless tenacity saw an average of 10 gigs a month, but in exceptional months, 15-20.

The phone bill also came in! In just one quarter, it was £600 ($800), and we sat around my grubby flat wondering how the hell we were going to pay it. In 1989, you paid for every call. There were no unlimited bundles.

The operating costs kept rising, unsurprisingly maybe. The more you do, the more it costs, but the key issue was that despite all the gigs the lads were doing, we made little to no money. In some cases, it cost us money.

The other problem was that no one wanted to pay much for a band playing their original material. So, we had to get creative.

We first had to get regular money for general expenses, including astronomical phone bills. To cover this, the band agreed to play the working men's club circuit so we could focus on what we needed to do.

Working men's clubs are a type of private social club first created in the 19th century in industrialised areas of Britain, particularly the North of England, the Midlands, Scotland and many parts of the South Wales Valleys. They were created to provide recreation for working-class men and their families.

The folks who frequent these places often were ashen-faced, disinterested, or pissed drunk out of their minds. The band would sometimes be an inconvenient distraction holding up the next game of bingo.

But some bands played this circuit of clubs quite seriously. They travelled with professional sound systems and lights and tried to look the part. For the Troubleshooters, it was a means to an end. Each gig paid between £125-£200 per show, so it was possible to have £600-£800 a month coming in to underwrite the costs of the 'real' band.

Phone bill. Paid.

This foundation helped us be more creative. With a bedrock of gigs, the next steps were getting onto the radio and piercing London. But even with the foundation we laid, it wasn't enough to fund additional activities.

One of the regular venues the band played was called The Kazbah, and the manager was a fan of the band. I put it to him that if he advanced the money for four shows from the band (they were scheduled to play anyway), then we'd release a single on his 'Kazbah Records' label.

With ego massaged, the cheque got cut the week after. The single got cut the month after that.

'One Day At A Time' was a cheery pop-rock number that bounced along and became the leading song of a AA side single. These were still the days of music being released on vinyl. The budget was so tight that we got a band friend who worked in a print shop to design the artwork in Letraset, a dry lettering transfer method. Think sticky letters for grown-ups. He physically stuck letters on some cards and took a photo of them.

What this single did do was give the band a focal point beyond the gig circuit. It was something we could approach radio stations with, something more impressive to send to booking agents and something that would make us generally look more serious and credible.

Five hundred copies got pressed, and about 100 were kept for promo. The promo copies got put to work and landed the band spots on local radio, press and some better gigs with bigger audiences. This kind of activity started producing a broader awareness of the band as their reputation as one of the hardest-working bands in the North East grew.

The trick now was to carry it on and take it up a level. Fortunately for me, The Sunderland Festival was coming up, and the council authorities were running a competition to appear on a big music festival bill with Jools Holland (a well-known TV music personality and member of the hit British band Squeeze).

We won a place on the bill, but more than that, I managed to convince the council authorities that the Sunderland Festival needed a theme song from Sunderland's premier up-and-coming band. And that they should pay for it.

And so, the band's second single was confirmed.

'With You All The Way' was a very different affair from the first single. It had a glossier production, well-designed artwork (on a computer this time), and more extensive support for the record as it was the official theme song for the Sunderland Festival. So, locally, it underpinned the band's position.

The Festival concert itself was a big outdoor event on the riverside, and the Troubleshooters were in support of Jools Holland. The band relished getting on a big concert stage with a big audience. What no one had factored in was that it would rain. A lot. And so, the audience didn't stick around.

Regardless, the lads enjoyed themselves so much on the big stage, and it was a great opportunity to see them play outside of a club setting. And they excelled.

At this point, I had London on my mind. With two singles in my briefcase, I had a story to tell of a band making waves in their home region. So I hit the phones, and the phone bill hit me right back as Sunderland to London was considered long-distance calling in those days.

I cold called. Nothing but the cold shoulder. I sent a handful of the band's singles to target publishers and record labels with a decent press pack that had a whiff of momentum about the band. Left it a week and then hit the phones again.

I got a few meetings and blagged my way around the major labels but didn't get any traction. But one meeting did stand out.

KEY LESSONS IN
LIFE AND BUSINESS

YOU NEED MORE WHEN YOU REALISE YOU CAN MATCH YOUR PASSION WITH YOUR ABILITY TO DO IT

I couldn't just stand still. My life away from touring wasn't enough because I'd proven I could do it. I realised that to grow, I needed to carry on reproving myself.

THE BEST PRODUCT DOESN'T ALWAYS WIN

When the band didn't win the battle of the band's competition, it was a travesty. It taught me that the best bands and products aren't always the most popular ones or the ones that get chosen.

SOMETIMES YOU MAKE DUMB DECISIONS

Agreeing to manage the band made absolutely no sense, no sense whatsoever. So, of course, I said yes. I took a leap of faith. It seemed like a dumb decision at the time, but years later, it became a brilliant decision.

MAKE STUFF HAPPEN BEYOND ALL THE ODDS

This has been a recurring theme in my career. People say, "when you think about Harvey Lee, he gets shit done." I manage to do things other people can't. Sometimes, it's just about being prepared to try something.

When I was younger, I could take leaps of faith more often. Now I can't because I'm so data-driven and have too many responsibilities and commitments. So really, the timing has to be right.

CHAPTER 12

TAKIN' CARE OF BUSINESS

"**W**ould you like a coffee, Harvey?" Peter Knight Jnr asked, with a smile.

"Sure, thank you," I said as I gazed at the gold discs on the wall behind him.

"I'll be right back," he replied. Then he pottered off to the downstairs kitchen. We were in his North London townhouse.

I enjoyed two minutes of absorbing the ambience of the room. The gold discs, photos, books, and lots of vinyl records all added to it.

Peter Knight Jnr had handled the publishing of many of the greatest artists in the world, and I was nervous. He'd worked with Quincy Jones, John Denver, Thelonious Monk, Charles Aznavour, and Charles Trenet, to name just a few. He'd run successful record companies with artists including Black Sabbath, Marianne Faithfull, Small Faces, and Alex Corner. At Polydor, where he was in charge of A&R, he worked with The Bee Gees, Jimi Hendrix, and, ironically, The Who.

"So, Harvey, it's the moment of truth; let's hear what the Troubleshooters have got..." he said as he handed me my coffee.

I was so nervous I almost spilt it.

Peter pressed play. I held my breath. And my buttocks.

It pounded out of the speakers. Peter stayed standing, conducting an invisible orchestra with his hands to the arrangement and tempo of the song.

I wasn't sure whether to laugh or join in!

He certainly wasn't afraid to show how he felt about the music. He was so animated and listened all the way through, unlike most of the record labels and publishers I'd met so far, who'd been dead behind their eyes.

"They're not the finished article, Harvey, but I'd like to come and see them play," Peter said as we shook hands. As I left the townhouse, the briefcase full of 7" records and demo tapes didn't seem so heavy.

But how was I going to get Peter to see the band play?

It was a bit of a stretch to get him to travel 275 miles to Sunderland from London, but I did manage to get the band on a 'new bands' bill at the Bull & Gate venue in North London. The venue was well-known for having six unknown bands every night.

The model was simple, you had to buy and resell the tickets to your fans. The venue wanted each band to bring a minimum guaranteed number of people, presumably so that they could sell them incredibly overpriced beer.

The Troubleshooters didn't have any fans in London. It was going to cost us a fortune to buy all the tickets, pay logistics costs for the band and pay to get a few fans to London. We just couldn't afford to do it.

Until it wasn't! I started thinking creatively about how we could find a solution. I made a list of the things we needed. It looked like this:

- Get the band, equipment and two roadies to London.
- Get some of the band's fans to travel on their own money, 275 miles to London, and

- Sell the tickets for the show and recoup the money we'd laid out.

Within a few minutes, I had an idea. After a few phone calls, I put it to the band.

"Lads, let's hire a 56-seater coach and sell tickets," I proposed.

"We can get at least 45 fans on the coach, band plus crew." I added, "The best bit about it is the proposition. 'A day out with the Troubleshooters in London for only £12 same-day return. See the sights of London and the Troubleshooter's first gig in London."

The coach sold out just by word of mouth. The gig, a somewhat chaotic affair we'd subsequently learn, was usual for the Bull and Gate. It came and went, as did Peter Knight.

We all felt something tangible would come from the first London music biz person coming to a show. Peter and I had a good chat after, and he clearly liked the band, but felt they were not quite developed enough for him to be involved.

However, we agreed to keep the communication lines open, and he wanted to be kept up-to-speed on the band's progress. So, I did my part.

A pattern began to emerge. My six-hour bus rides to London became more frequent to see record labels and music publishers, and the number of gigs the band played there increased. It all served the narrative in Sunderland that the Troubleshooters were going places.

There was a certain irony to one meeting I had.

Mickie Most was a prolific music producer from the 1960s until the mid-1980s.

Most was both talented and lucky – seeing Newcastle rhythm and blues outfit The Animals playing in London, he signed them to EMI on the condition that he was their producer. Their second single, 'House of The Rising Sun', released in the summer of 1964, proved an instant classic and topped both the UK and US pop charts.

In the late 1960s, rock music took on a new direction, and Most didn't adapt well. He learned that his tastes weren't in tune with rock fans, so he stuck with producing pop for the rest of his life.

Most created RAK Records and RAK Publishing at the end of the sixties. And in the early 1970s, RAK Records scored consistent UK hits with The Sweet, Smokey, Mud, and Suzi Quatro.

He became a household name.

The 'hit rate' in the 1980s found Most scoring success less often, although Hot Chocolate, Racey, Kim Wilde, and Johnny Hates Jazz all achieved some degree of popularity in the UK.

Yet, despite all this, his most phenomenal success was with **Herman's Hermits**. Yes! Herman's Hermits!

I felt like I was owed a meeting just because I had one degree of separation from him.

"Hello, RAK," said the expensive-sounding female voice down the phone.

"Good morning. Could I speak with Mickie Most, please?" I said with confidence.

"Who's calling?" enquired Mickie's human shield.

"It's Harvey Lee, a colleague of Herman's Hermits," I said expectantly.

Then silence.

"Hello, is that Harvey? This is Mickie."

Shit! I'm through, fucking compose yourself, I thought to myself. I hadn't expected it to be that easy.

"Hi Mickie, this is Harvey, how are you?" I said in my most clear speaking voice, usually reserved for speaking to people in authority and my Grandmother on the phone.

"I've not had a phone call about Herman's Hermits for a

very long time, how are they?" he replied with an unexpectedly friendly tone.

I told him a slightly varnished version of the truth and the real reason I was calling. I think he felt slightly hoodwinked by how I got through to speak to him but being who he was, I think he just accepted that I should get credit for breaking through his barrier.

Getting through to people in the music business in London on the phone, when you are effectively nobody, is nigh on an impossible task, but it was something I was mastering. You only needed to give me 0.005% of a story about anything, and I'd use it to kick someone's door down – metaphorically speaking, of course.

So, I got the meeting with Mickie.

When the day came, I stood in front of the very imposing RAK Studios building in the St. Johns Wood area of London, well known for being home to foreign ambassadors, with my black attaché case, blazer and demo tape, ready to talk turkey.

Man, the building was an alabaster column-fronted mansion – literally, an ambassador's residence. I rang the buzzer and waited for the high-rent walking human shield to grant me access.

Standing in the lobby of RAK, you could see, feel, and smell the money. It was more White House than Roadhouse, but who cared? Success was in the air! I was led up the long curving staircase by some super-model type and to the door of what would be Mickie's office.

Gold and Platinum discs seemed to be wallpapered everywhere.

The walk from the door to his desk seemed to take four years. Sitting in a high-backed, expensive leather chair, he had his back to me as I approached his desk. Then he slowly swivelled around to reveal himself.

Mickie, come on, it's a music meeting; you're not a James Bond villain! But he *was* playing the role of music impresario to the full. Halfway through the 'swivel', his legs came up off the floor, he crossed them mid-air and his feet, clad in expensive cowboy boots, landed on his desk as he leaned back.

Could he have been any more of a stereotypical music mogul?

"Hey, what do you have for me?" he said cordially.

We chatted, and I played the tape. He skipped through each song after 30-60 seconds and rejected everything roundly. I should have expected that a bubble-gum pop impresario would react to a rock band like that.

I never saw Mickie Most again, but I did repeat the one-degree-of-separation trick to open doors of influential people again in the years to come.

Back 'up North', we were in the perpetual motion of gigs that became full-blown tours. Very tricky logistically as two of the band had full-time jobs and families to look after.

So many challenges and so many memories I'll never forget, like the time when the band's van rolled backwards on an incline towards a straight drop over a small cliff. As it moved past driverless, we all looked at each other as it overtook us and Kevin, the drummer, shouted, "Harvey, man!"

Part and parcel of being a manager is taking the blame. Even if it was the drummer who forgot to put the handbrake on.

A local paper once wrote that the band was managed by 'the very famous Harvey Lee.' I was sarcastically introduced as "the very famous..." from thereon in by the band – just more cannon fodder to feed the crack.

Another memorable gig was when the band supported Aswad (a hit British Reggae band) at Chesterfield football ground. There was a 30,000 capacity... but we (and Aswad) played to less than 200 people. The promoter went bankrupt... that sound familiar? It can happen to the best of them!

There were also many broken-down vans, very hot curries, little sleep, and real financial hardship. They were all contributing factors to the shared vision and goal, the commitment, the hard work, the togetherness, and the friendship.

But ultimately, it all ended in tears. And I ended my part in it. Badly.

From my perspective, I wasn't mature enough to admit to myself that I'd failed. I felt like I was letting the band down and was consumed with guilt about leaving them.

As emotions ran high, I must've fumbled my announcement to the band somewhat, but despite the surprise, they saw I couldn't take it anymore.

They were more than understanding. Whatever had happened, we'd been through more together in two years than most would in a lifetime. The leaving party in my flea pit was something to behold. I thought that place couldn't have looked worse than it already did. I was wrong. Very wrong.

But despite this chapter closing, a familiar one was re-opening.

KEY LESSONS IN LIFE AND BUSINESS

BE CREATIVE IN SOLVING PROBLEMS

Richard Branson is quoted as saying, "Launching a business is essentially an adventure in problem-solving."

And boy, did I have problems to solve. From getting a fan-base 275 miles to a one-off show in London on a budget, to cracking the doors open of London's music industry to having to pay that enormous phone bill.

At the heart of everything was creativity. If I'd tried to do everything by the book, nothing would have happened.

DO THE JOB YOU WANT

Do the job you want, as well as the job you *have* to do. The job I had was booking the band on the club circuit to pay my phone bill, but the job I wanted was sitting in Mickie Most's chair behind his desk. So, I went about being that persona, and it worked. It opened doors.

THE TROUBLESHOOTERS

▲ The Troubleshooters wowed at the 1988 Yarm Festival. It was clear early on that they excelled on stage.

► Messing about in the recording studio in Hull, North Yorkshire, 1989.

CHAPTER 13

THE LONG AND WINDING ROAD

"**H**arvey, Ray's asking for you. He won't do the tour without *you* on the side of the stage with him," exclaimed the promoter down the phone.

I seriously doubted that, but I needed to put the Troubleshooters behind me, so I hit the road harder than ever, knowing I'd just be getting on the hamster wheel of touring again. Maybe it'd do me good?

After another month with Herman's Hermits, I joined another band on the road that had been huge in the 70s and 80s, Dr. Hook.

Dr. Hook were mostly remembered for their disco hits 'When You're In Love With A Beautiful Woman' and 'Sexy Eyes', but at their core, they were a country band from the American South.

The original band was fronted by Dennis Locorriere and Ray 'Eye Patch' Sawyer, and they too had had an acrimonious break up in the band resulting in Dennis and Ray going their separate ways.

In a sense of déjà vu, there were *two* Dr. Hooks! Ray won the rights to the name and toured under the name 'Dr. Hook' and

Dennis had to tour under the moniker of 'Dennis Locorriere, the voice of Dr. Hook.'

I was on tour with Ray, so *just* 'Dr. Hook.' Ray had won the right to use the name in its plain and simple guise as he was considered the 'visual identity of the band.'

Just add a cowboy hat, boots, maracas and an old-fashioned 'pirate' eye patch, and you have the visual ID of Ray Sawyer. It's the main visible thing that people remember about the band.

Dennis was *just* the voice. But it wasn't enough to win the outright usage of the name at the time, even though in the latter years of their biggest successes, he took over the lead vocals from Ray.

In quick succession, I did three tours with Dr. Hook in the UK and Ireland. The standout tour was in 1992 when EMI Records released a compilation called 'Completely Hooked, the best of Dr. Hook.' With the backing of TV advertising, it peaked at number three on the UK charts and spent 22 weeks in the top 100. Eight of those weeks were in the top 40.

The tour was in October, and off the success of the album, it was in bigger venues (theatres, not clubs) and sold out well in advance.

However, managing Ray was everyone's pet challenge because:

1. He was quite deaf
2. Substance consumption was rife

He wouldn't wear his hearing aids, and as the monitoring engineer responsible for helping the band hear themselves on stage, you got put to the sword. Every single night.

Ray insisted on extra loud monitoring of his voice on stage. Usually, a lead singer would get two floor monitors around the position of their microphone. Ray had six on the floor and an eight-foot standing monitor on each side of the stage.

Only Ray's voice was allowed to come out of any of these

speakers at a deafeningly loud volume. The deaf person was making everyone else deaf!

And, if Ray wasn't happy, regardless of how loud it was, we had to turn it up some more until everything would start feeding back (sonic screeching).

Then, there were the artist's tantrums. If you could, you'd run away when you saw the signs.

My worst job was when it was my turn for the 'Bob' run. One night, at the Empire Theatre in Liverpool, Ray turned to the tour manager and asked who had Bob.

Bob, as it turns out, was not a person. Bob Hope *was* a person in this context. Bob Hope is rhyming slang for rope. The rope is dope. Dope is... illegal!

Every night on this tour, Ray's 'stash' had to be checked into the central hotel safe, not the safe in your room. That would be too incriminating to the individual. The crew took turns looking after this task, and it was my turn in Liverpool.

Despite being illegal, the task was simple.

Go to the reception desk, ask to deposit a small cardboard box in the hotel safe, put your name on it and collect it later. And try to keep clean underwear until it's someone else's turn.

Everything would have been much easier if Ray had put his hearing aids in and stayed off the naughty stuff.

Over the next few years, I toured a lot with Herman's Hermits, especially in America. One year I toured the States three times, not including a one-off gig in Austin, Texas, when I flew there from Britain for a day to do the show and then flew straight back.

The Manchester music scene had become hot at this point, and what would soon be known as the 'Brit-pop' movement was sprouting after its earlier seedling stage.

But I wasn't progressing, and I needed a change.

One gig at Manchester University in the very early 90s convinced me that this change had to come sooner rather than later.

The La's were a very hyped indie band from Liverpool, with a hit single behind them in 'There She Goes.' They were *very* hot for a while. But their constant line-up changes and troubles were well documented.

I came to work with them and witnessed them implode.

At sound check, they were difficult. I was doing on-stage monitoring and checking through their (unreasonable) demands in the afternoon, which was hard enough. Come showtime, they went on stage an hour late to an audience who were already impatient, but worse still, they were out of their heads… assumed drunk, but the effects could've been way beyond alcohol.

Before they even sang a note, they decided to walk on stage and re-arrange all their equipment so that all the sound settings from the afternoon's sound check made no sense. And all this in front of their own audience.

They sounded terrible. They cut their set short (mercifully for the rest of us) and then proceeded to have a massive, drunken argument in their dressing room.

That year, they officially broke up. Mismanagement seemed not just to be rife in the 60s and 70s, but the 90s too.

I was busy, really busy, but I wasn't making enough money to sustain a life back home. I was still *having* to live with my parents. I was away so much that time at home was limited, but none of this was insurmountable. I *could've* taken my touring career to the next level, but I didn't because I knew I'd be in it for life if I did.

I didn't want to be on the road forever; I wanted to work in the *business* of music. But this wouldn't happen living on the road – or at my parent's house. I'd tried this before, though, and it had ended in tears. This time around, there was a key difference in my thinking.

Learn the lessons. Apply the learnings.

And then, a turn of fate. A demo tape showed up at my house.

The black front cover said 'Smalltown Heroes.' Who the fuck were the Smalltown Heroes?

Reading the inlay, I saw that the line-up looked familiar: it was the Troubleshooters! They'd changed their name. And it seemed their music too. It'd improved dramatically.

After what I might surmise was a ton of soul-searching after I left, they'd decided to carry on. The band had been in creative development, with Peter Knight Jnr playing an increasingly active role. He'd funded new demos and was advising the band.

The result was a demo tape that stood up and made you take notice, the title track 'Moral Judgement' especially. Then, the phone call.

"Hey Harv, how're things?" said Baz.

"Hey, Baz. Good to hear from you," I replied. Despite not managing the band anymore and leaving them a couple of years prior, we'd always stayed in close contact.

"We've had some cracking news. We won a competition. We're going to support the Little Angels at Newcastle City Hall," he revealed.

"Wow, that's great, made up for you, man. A bit different from playing to 100 people in Sinatra's bar in Sunderland!" I was thrilled for them.

"Sure is. There'll be over 2,000 people there. We'd love you to be there too," he added.

"I wouldn't miss it for the world," I replied. And I meant it. If anyone deserved a break, it was them.

Two weeks later, it was show time.

The band blew the theatre's back wall out, raised the roof, got the audience on their feet, and did a brisk business of selling demo tapes on the official merchandise concession stand afterwards.

"Harvey, ol' boy, how are you?" Peter Knight greeted me like a long-lost friend. He'd ventured 275 miles from London to see the results of his investment.

"Peter," I blurbed... then the bromantic embrace.

We chatted about the band (away from the band), then cracked open a tinny (can of beer) backstage with the lads, who were justifiably in a triumphant mood and on a well-earned high.

They were the best version of themselves I'd ever seen in every respect, but the same perpetual problem existed. They were the big fish in the very small pond. They still needed to break out, and all the same barriers were in place.

Everything had changed, yet nothing had changed.

The next day, in a pub on Newcastle Road, Sunderland, we sat around and talked quite soberly and honestly about the challenges. And it came to pass that the band were still keen to work with me. They'd seen what I could do on my own.

We all agreed that the critical part was learning from the past.

They needed a manager with some clout in London. I needed and wanted to move to London to be closer to the business of music. Creative solutions were needed, and they came to me.

We set out an agreement in simple terms:

- [band] Harvey, we want you to manage us, but you need to have the backing of a more prominent manager or an existing management company.
- [me] Yes, I agree.
- [band] We have an offer of a Publishing Deal with Global Music on the table, but on its own, it's not yielded any interest in the industry.
- [me] I know how to leverage it.

And so, the proposal was as follows. I went back to Manchester and kept doing road work, but in my spare time, I'd moonlight as the band's manager to get the band signed to a reputable management company on the basis that they'd hire me too.

It was my very own job creation scheme. But one that'd get me to where I wanted to be. In London.

And so, we parted on this agreement. It was all down to me to make it happen, and the band would carry on doing what they were doing, booking their own gigs.

My 'office' was a corner of my single bedroom at my parent's house. It comprised of humble tools of the era:

- An electric typewriter
- A fax machine
- A bottle of Tippex (because I was not a very good typist!)

I got hold of a copy of the White Book, the UK music business directory of the day, and decided to fax hundreds of music management companies to lure them into a meeting without even hearing or knowing the band.

The faxed letter went something like this...

A **Fax Transmission from Shekel Music**

Dear (music person I want something out of),

I'm the manager of Smalltown Heroes, which has (list notable achievements) recently culminated in the band getting signed to a publishing deal with Global Music Limited.

The band are yet to receive their advance (money in advance in lieu of future royalties), but their recording rights are still open, and I'm looking to join a management company to take the band to.

I'll be in London the week of (whenever you want me there) and would love the opportunity to discuss this commercial venture with you in more detail.

Blah blah, Harvey Lee.

Let me translate this fax into motivations and actions:

1. Key message: The band have got a publishing deal. Translation: they're not unsigned losers, and half the pre-work is done for you.
2. Key message: They haven't had their advance yet. Translation: you get a percentage as commission, and you've not missed the boat, even though you did nothing to earn it.
3. Key message: They have a competent manager. Translation: you only have to give me a desk and a modest salary, and I'll do all the work.
4. Key message: I'm looking to join a management company. Translation: the band will be contracted to you, not me. I'll work for you. You get the benefits of post-contract royalties; I won't.

The music business is a community driven by trends and fads. If a hot young band is attracting some heat, the labels, publishers, and the like will be attracted to that heat with the simple laws of attraction at play. This fax played straight into the hands of anyone who bothered to read it.

There was a bit of an IT problem, however. I had no incoming fax number, so how would I receive my replies? Imagine if some Mickie Most-type rang up and got my mum answering the phone? It couldn't be allowed to happen.

So, I found a local print shop with a fax service and agreed that I would use their fax number for incoming faxes. They'd call me if anything came in.

In a flurry of activity from my bedroom, there must've been hundreds of these things going out. I occasionally had to turn the fax machine off as it overheated. Then, I waited. And waited.

How long would I have to wait before I got a bite? A week? Two weeks? Would I get a bite? It was my whole strategy, if no leads came from these faxes, I'd effectively got no other cards to play. It would be a touring life for me. Then...

"Hello, Harvey? It's Jack at the print shop. You've got some faxes here waiting for you from London."

I don't think I said anything in reply; I just dropped the phone and ran to the shop!

Within three days, I got six faxes back. Three 'Dear John' rejections, one of which thanked me for submitting my demo (read the fax before you reply, dickhead!), and three genuine enquiries.

They were from:

1. Premier Talent. A very big concert booking agency.
2. Prince Rupert Lowenstein. The infamous Rolling Stones financier.
3. EG Music Group. A well-known and successful independent music company.

All three expressed interest and requested a meeting, but the reply from EG Music Group was the most interesting. It read something like this:

```
Dear Harvey,

Thank you for, yada yada. Sounds very inter-
esting, yadda yadda.

I know Peter Knight Jnr and the Global Music
Group very well and have spoken to him about
the band. Please call my office to arrange a
meeting with me here.

More pleasantries,

Sam Alder.
Chairman. EG Music Group
```

Jackpot! This was meaningful!

So, calls went in, meetings were arranged, and I was off to London on the train.

The meeting with Premier Talent was a very uncommitted fishing meeting. They just wanted to know when the band would likely get a record deal. Their interest was based on the fact that they didn't want to miss out on anything. The fact that they'd not even listened to the tape I sent them showed that they were going through the motions.

Lowenstein was more interesting. I didn't meet the 'Prince' himself, but I did go to his office, which seemed like a palace fit for the Bavarian aristocrat that he actually was. His staff were attentive and genuinely interested, had listened to the music and wanted to know what the deal would look like with me on board. Ending cordially, we agreed to keep in touch.

I had my eyes on the prize, the meeting with EG.

You'll have never heard of EG unless you're over 50 years old and were heavily involved in the music industry in the 70s and 80s. However, you *will* have heard of some of their artists. Marc Bolan of T-Rex, King Crimson, Emerson Lake and Palmer (ELP), Killing Joke, and probably most famous of all...Roxy Music and Brian Ferry.

EG was a creative powerhouse across management, publishing and production for two decades. Well-known for developing artists, they had the creative integrity that artists like but, through licencing arrangements initially with Island Records, then Polydor Records and latterly, Richard Branson's Virgin Records, the commercial reach to turn artistic integrity into commercial success.

Before I even walked in the door, I believed this was the right home for the band. And, for me.

I pressed the buzzer on number 63a Kings Road, the swanky

address of their Georgian townhouse office. Walking into reception, all the gold and platinum discs for some of the artists previously mentioned wallpapered the walls. They stared down at me as if they were sending me a message. If the discs could've talked, they would have said:

"If you're coming here, you'd *better* be bringing hit records."

I was under so much pressure. This meeting was the best tangible lead I had. I had one shot.

"Sam will see you now," said his PA and she escorted me into his office.

Sam Alder was a different proposition from anyone I'd met in the business yet. As far as I was concerned, he was a heavyweight.

"Harvey, Sam Alder, how are you? Great to meet you," Sam said.

My first impression of Sam was that he looked like a well-heeled private banker, minus the cigar.

He had silver hair, a well-cut suit, braces, and a cut-glass English-speaking voice. He fostered a well-cultivated exterior, but there was a steely determination about him. Sam had a twinkle in his eyes; one twinkle was for a business opportunity, the other twinkle was for the ladies.

His jovial, warm and welcoming demeanour melted away any sense of intimidation or nerves I might've had. Peter was also in the room, he'd arrived earlier than me and had a 'pre-meeting' with Sam. Karen, EG's A&R representative, was also present.

In Sam's classic old-fashioned gentleman's club of an office sat four people, a pot of fresh coffee, and very high expectations.

I sat and listened intently to what Sam had to say. *His pitch* was that EG were re-booting after selling their catalogues to the media giant BMG Publishing (not to be confused with the BMG of today) and Richard Branson's Virgin Records.

He was on the lookout for what was next for EG. His partner, Mark Fenwick, had stepped back from EG after the catalogue sale but had kept his hand in the business by managing Roger Waters of Pink Floyd fame.

And then the penny dropped. I saw what Sam saw. An opportunity to nurture a new band to get EG back in the game as an independent with no specific ties to a major label anymore.

Given that Smalltown Heroes were already partly developed and packaged, would *they* be the band that Sam Alder would want to help him in *his* quest?

KEY LESSONS IN LIFE AND BUSINESS

DON'T BE STUPID

It's often said once said that "the definition of insanity is doing the same thing over and over and expecting different results."

I knew that if I had a crack at managing the band a second time, we'd have to change the conditions and the context, or the results would be the same.

A move to London could only happen if I went to work for a more prominent manager or artist management company. The band would get what they justifiably needed, and I'd get what I wanted, i.e. a start in the business of music, in the epicentre of music. London.

USE THE PAST TO SHAPE THE FUTURE

Smalltown Heroes had learnt from the past.

They'd developed and reinvented themselves. They'd realised they couldn't keep doing the same things repeatedly. They'd realised they needed to reposition themselves as a harder-edged rock band, with tighter arrangements and a focus on great melody to prove it in the market.

STORYTELLING IS YOUR SECRET WEAPON TO CUT THROUGH

When I sent out all the faxes, it was about the creation of a story from the assets I had to work with. I used the improved tale of the band to entice interest from a specific target audience, the artist management companies. I explained that they had a publishing deal but hadn't received the money yet, so there were plenty of opportunities.

It wasn't the band's musical story, that cut sway. It was the business story of the band, which is all that management companies care about. A deal was in the bag and would open the door to others.

You must ensure you're telling the right story, at the right time, to the right audience.

LIKE IT OR NOT, LIKE ATTRACTS LIKE

The law of attraction plays very strongly in business. I knew that if one credible person from the music industry were committed to our band, others would be as well. They're like sheep. One walks through the paddock gates, and the rest follow. If you've had no interest, then no one wants to know. Baaa.

The funny thing is that EG had passed up on the band two years previously. Their former A&R guy had travelled up to Manchester to see them, liked them, but passed on them. He wasn't there anymore, but the chairman of the same company was now interested as the context for EG had changed.

If you do the right things, don't give up, and work smart, you'll create that little bit of luck we all need from time to time.

CHAPTER 14

LONDON CALLING

"**H**arvey, I like what I hear, I like what I see, I like you, now I want to see it for myself," Sam said directly.

I nodded.

"I can't decide anything more now. To do that, I need to see the band play live," he finished. He stood up as if to say, the meeting's over, homeboy.

Sam Alder laid it all out in the meeting. If he decided to sign the band, then I'd go to work for him and the EG Music Group. Ultimately, however, his decision would hinge on a showcase, and the band *had* to play a concert in London. If he liked what he saw, a deal would formally be offered; if he didn't, we'd lose the whole thing.

It was like Julius Caesar at the Colosseum in Rome. Thumbs up, and we'd get to live; thumbs down, we'd be dead. Or at least the current vision of our future would be.

Setting up a show in London, especially for an unsigned, unknown band, wasn't easy. Even though I spent a week on the phone, I couldn't find a spot on a bill anywhere in London for the next three months. And I couldn't risk EG going cold on the band, the deal was hot *now*.

We wanted to play in front of an audience so EG could see the band's magic. However, it was evident that this wouldn't happen anytime soon, so the decision made itself.

We had to pay to hire a venue and put on a private showcase ourselves.

Not only would this cost be a bitter and expensive pill to swallow, an industry showcase is usually a behind-closed-doors affair with no audience but the invited guests. It's cold, impersonal and often done at a rehearsal facility.

This wasn't the experience or the light we wanted our guests to see the band in. So, we decided together that we'd seek to put on a FULL show with a powerful sound system, lights, and the works.

To just six industry people. In the daytime.

The band had played the Mean Fiddler club in North London a few times and generally had a good experience with the venue, sound system and, critically, audiences. So, it seemed like the obvious choice.

It was also a well-known venue in the industry. A&R (Artist & Repertoire) folks from record labels, publishers and the like were happy to go there. It made perfect sense.

And just like most businesses, they don't turn down easy money. So, when it came to a 'dry hire' during the day, we could almost pick our date. After a few calls, back-and-forth, the date was set.

You could sense the apprehension, excitement, and trepidation on the day of the showcase.

Everything went to plan in the set-up, and then we waited. Moreover, we waited for Sam and the other EG folks to turn up.

Finally, as if it were the most natural thing in the world, they walked in, all smiles, cordial greetings and expectations. I calmly walked backstage to see the band to tell them that it was time. I never gave the band pep talks because they never needed them.

I decided to do nothing notably different. I didn't want to put additional pressure on them. I just wished them a great show and to do what they do and enjoy it.

It was broad daylight outside, but inside it was dark like any night-time concert, and you could feel the heat of the beaming stage lights around the venue. The band walked on stage and launched into a 45-minute show.

The lads switched off from the reality of the situation and just focused on what was important. Playing as if their lives depended on it was their default setting. Being submerged into the experience of this show, after the first song, I think *we all* forgot there was no audience.

We might as well have been playing a sold-out show at the Hollywood Bowl. The artificial circumstances rapidly dwindled into irrelevance.

And this is where all those hundreds of shows the band had played paid off. It was this moment. All that experience, all the tough gigs, the crap gigs, the brilliant gigs, the band intuitively pulled on all of that. And then steamrollered the showcase.

At one point, they even tried to get the industry folks to participate in a sing-along! They knew they *did* have an audience – an audience of one. Sam Alder was the only person in the room that mattered.

When all was said and done, band dripping with sweat and relief, the daytime house lights went back on, and it was time for the reckoning. The band, expecting. They had done their job.

It didn't come.

Not then and there, and I could say, after everything, I understood the band's evident angst. They'd done everything that'd been asked of them, but the immediate verbal commitment from EG that was expected wasn't forthcoming.

This was mainly down to our unrealistic expectations. You hear stories of old that go, "yeah, I signed them on the spot," as if some music impresario pulled a contract out of their arse in the dressing room.

If they even existed, those days were long gone. Contracts, negotiations, and commitments were all legally accountable, and there was a process. I had some crumbs of comfort for the band. Well, more than crumbs.

Sam was very encouraging, and the band and I were invited to the EG office for a meeting the next day. You weren't usually invited in like this if you're going to get rejected; no one wants to waste their time.

So, I asked Sam to go backstage and speak with the band directly as a gesture of goodwill to initiate the relationship and forge bonds.

The crunch came the following afternoon at 63a Kings Road, Chelsea. Kings Road is a very famous address. It was the centre of fashion and music in the 1960s.

For most artists, especially ones that have never been signed before, a meeting like this is where you learn your fate.

So, here we all were sitting in the boardroom. Expecting. Band, Peter Knight from Global Music and myself. We were waiting on Sam to start.

"I have to tell you that I thoroughly enjoyed your show yesterday, and you only confirmed what I had suspected all along," opened Sam. "You have a bright future and a great team in Harvey and Peter... I want EG to be a big part of that team," he initially concluded.

The atmospheric pressure in the room immediately rolled back to something approaching normal.

"We're going to offer you a management contract with the EG Music Group. You'll be signed to us, Harvey will join EG as an employee and continue to be your manager with our backing," he continued.

"EG will work with Peter and Global Music to schedule recordings, and we'll seek to licence them out to another label."

Satisfied, Sam sat back in his chair and waited on the response.

"Aye, Sam, yer on man, that's fantastic, we can't wait!" the boys declared out loud, but the response was more visual and visceral than verbal. Years of toil had led to this moment, a moment where mere words were not sufficient.

The band would be put on an essential retainer and could go full-time. The contract would be for three years with options for further years.

We'd done it!

The joy and the relief were palpable. For me, it was mostly relief and validation of what the lads and I had believed and worked towards. This band deserved a real shot.

After a very drunken night of celebrations and shenanigans that shall stay in the 'what goes on tour stays on tour' folder, it was back to business. The lads went back to Sunderland and me, Manchester. Only, I had to plan my relocation to London with near-immediate effect.

As I sat on the train, thinking through everything that had happened and needed to happen, I felt a glaring stare from across the carriage aisle. Two fellas, looking at me, were talking between themselves, clearly talking about me. They were checking my Anvil flight-case briefcase out, hardly subtle. Maybe they were going to mug me? One of them seemed to have one giant eyebrow across his forehead!

They were both quite distinctive looking, but I'd never seen them before and thought nothing of it. Until I put the TV on that night to see them both performing on the Tops of the Pops, the most famous music show in the country. The slow-mid tempo rock drawl went...

"I need to be myself."
"I can't be no one else."
"I'm feeling supersonic."

Fuck me, it was Oasis! I sat across the aisle from Noel and Liam Gallagher from Oasis and said absolutely nothing. I thought they looked like they were about to mug me, but I would come to learn that that's how they always looked!

Between my two management stints of the band, whilst I was touring elsewhere, the band had struck up a close working partnership with a couple of aspiring producers, Marshall Bird and Steve Bush (professionally known as Bird & Bush).

Through Steve's work connections, he had access to down-time at Battery Studios and used the time to hone his skills and leverage to attract new bands to work with. Battery was renowned in the business, and some pretty big artists had been through there at the time. Bryan Adams, Robbie Williams, etc. Not too shabby!

I met Steve in the café of Battery as it was increasingly likely we'd be intertwined with our relationship with the band. And he was looking for a flatmate. No longer. I committed to the room as soon as he mentioned it. I might've taken it before he formally offered it.

I had no idea how I would make it pay in the short term, but I did have the (unsigned) EG deal in my metaphorical back pocket. And the week after, I bid my parents goodbye (again) and drove to London with almost everything I owned in the back of a van.

Plus, a box of 'essentials' from mum.

It felt amazing to be a London resident. From the very first day, I could feel the energy of this famous city and looking to the future seemed more important than the flea pit I'd just moved into. Admittedly, it was better than the apartment in Sunderland, but not by much.

My bedroom became my office (again!), and once things had settled, the contract finally arrived, and it was time to get the band legal representation. And a haircut.

For years, my long hair had been a point of pride, a visual sign of my place in the world. But in the past year or so, it had been getting shorter and shorter. I could no longer look like the road crew if I wanted to be managing the business of a band in London. One last 'snip', and it was collar length, not halfway down my back!

After meeting a few uninspiring music business lawyers, I settled on John Kennedy to represent the band.

When the band heard his client list, it was an easy sell. Band Aid, Live Aid, Stone Roses, Creation Records, and now, erm, Smalltown Heroes. He had a reputation for championing the artist, and after all I'd learnt in my time in the industry, a legal champion would be a welcome addition to the team.

So, when I told Sam Alder that John Kennedy would represent the band, his cordial indifference was barely noticeable.

"Hello Harvey, it's John Kennedy. I've read the EG contract…"

"OK, John – and?" I said on the phone, unsuspecting.

"It's got to be one of the worst contracts I've ever seen. Commission on gross, not net is just universally unacceptable in this day and age."

He continued to rattle off a few other key points that got lost on me as my world started to fall apart around me.

He red-lined it and sent it back to EG's lawyers.

The next phone call was from Sam Alder.

"Harvey, I'm fucking livid at John Kennedy, and I'm fucking livid at you. This is the deal, take it or leave it," Sam said abruptly. It'd seem Sam had a hard centre and soft outside.

As a manager, I always championed the band, but I wasn't on the inside yet, and that prospect was getting wobblier by the minute. I pushed for some concessions and explored areas of compromise, trying to get any changes of note.

And boy, did we get changes.

The phone line went dead without so much as a goodbye. What the fuck had just happened?

I called back and spoke to Karen, the A&R. She asked me what I'd said to Sam because he was uncharacteristically angry.

"I didn't mean to cause offence, Karen. I'm just doing my job," I said.

"OK, let me see what's going on, and I'll call you back," Karen said with a strong sense of trepidation.

Karen had been key to the whole deal. She'd been a champion for the band inside the company from the get-go. She'd invested months and months of work, partnering with me to make this deal happen. If anyone could help, it was her.

"Harvey, it's Karen. I have no idea what's happened, but Sam just told me to forget about the deal. He said there's plenty more fish in the sea. I'm so sorry, but it's all off," she said apologetically.

I put the phone down and slumped in my chair. I'd never been so desperately deflated. My life flashed before my eyes. I'd moved to London on the back of this deal, but in reality, I didn't have a penny to my name. The future I'd worked so hard to sculpt was in complete ruins.

How on earth would I approach this gargantuan shit sandwich with the band? I had to front it out and get to the point before my inevitable harpooning.

To say the news wasn't met well was the understatement of the century. The lads understandably went wild, but one thing was true. We were all in this together, and for better or worse, we had a decision to make.

Either accept the deal was off and risk the whole project breaking apart, or accept the agreement *against* our legal advice. Advice from the band's lawyer, for heaven's sake!

At the end of the day, it wasn't me signing the deal. It was the four members of the band. The cold, harsh reality of the situation decided for us. There was no other option if this band (and I) were going to continue.

They agreed amongst themselves to sign the deal, regardless of the concerns raised by their lawyer. Of course, there was a huge caveat to deciding to sign it. Would EG even still want the band? How could I get all that goodwill back and the contract back on the table after it all exploded?

There was no reasoned or logical way I thought I could play it.

For the first time, Sam Alder wouldn't take my call. I wanted to talk him through the key points and, critically, the outcome. But the option wasn't even available to me. I had to get in front of him right then and there. It was all happening in one afternoon, and I knew I couldn't let this go cold.

I figured that if he slept on it, things might be even more irretrievable. Feeling desperate, I engaged the only option left.

I begged.

It was the only way. I wrote a fax. Not typed on my trusty lucky electric Brother typewriter. A coarse handwritten note in thick black marker pen, in GIANT lettering. It read something like this:

DEAR SAM,

THE BAND WANTS TO SIGN THE DEAL AS IS. KISS ASS, BEG, KISS MORE ASS, DESPERATELY BEG SOME MORE, MAKING CLEAR THAT HE HAS ALL THE CARDS AND YOU'LL DO ANYTHING. LITERALLY.

HARVEY

I faxed it, and I called Karen.

"Karen, it's Harvey. I just sent a fax for Sam's urgent attention. Can you please, *please* ensure it gets to him?" I begged.

"Hold on, it's coming through now...OK, got it. I'm going to put it in front of him and see what he says," Karen said. "I'll call you back."

It was the longest 30 minutes of my life. I think I beat the world record for the number of individual cigarettes smoked in half an hour. As I lit up the eighth one, the phone rang. It was Karen.

"He said, OK. He can accept that the band would side with their lawyer's opinion, and he'll let it go. Let's get it signed and move on," Karen said with palpable relief.

Broken, I thanked Karen for everything she'd done to support us. The desperate note worked, and the deal was back on despite it taking years off my life expectancy. Not yet *signed,* but back *on.*

John Kennedy was royally pissed off when I told him, but to be fair to him, he re-stated his advice and said the choice was the bands.

I'll never truly know what made Sam react the way he did. However, I later realised a different dispute was playing out that might have had something to do with it.

KEY LESSONS IN LIFE AND BUSINESS

FOCUS ON PLAN A

We didn't have a Plan B. The showcase was career-defining for the band. It was the moment when the rubber hit the road. The talking stopped, and it was either going to work, or it wasn't. It didn't matter how much work we'd put into it.

None of us, myself included, had considered the fallout if it didn't work. Arnold Schwarzenegger did an interview called 'I Hate Plan B' – watch it on YouTube. It inspired millions and brought many to tears. In it, he says: "For me, it's hazardous to have a Plan B because you are cutting yourself off from the chance of really succeeding. People want to have a Plan B because they're worried about failing. What if I fail? Then I don't have anything else."

"Don't be afraid of failing because there's nothing wrong with failing. You have to fail to climb that ladder. No one doesn't fail."

Plan B didn't exist in our minds. It was like, "We must make this work. There's no choice." When the band walked onto the stage at the Mean Fiddler club, they switched off the reality of the situation and just focused on what was important.

That audience of one.

SOME THINGS AREN'T WHAT THEY SEEM, NOR ARE THEY FAIR

When the final recommendations came in from lawyer John Kennedy, it put everything at risk. It was a damning indictment of a contract offer we'd worked so hard to get. No one expected it to be so badly received by EG.

We were at risk of losing everything. I'd already moved to my flat in London, but things were not as straightforward as they should have been.

I had to grovel and take care of business. There was no Plan B; I had to save the situation (with Karen's help, of course!).

Over the years and through my corporate career, it's come to pass that the same is true; many things are not quite as they seem or as straightforward as they should be. We'd like to think we live in a meritocracy, but reality says otherwise.

Whether it be that promotion that always seems to elude you

or the 'bell curve' for compensation ratio where management *has to* give you a poorer review score than you deserve because 'too many people are 'good' and they can only fit a certain percentage into 'good'.

Life isn't fair, and things are rarely black and white. Ask questions. Lots and lots of questions.

CHAPTER 15

CHELSEA DAGGER

"**G**ather around, lads, you've got a contract to sign," I announced as the band took a break from recording demos at Battery Studios.

The day had finally come in the summer of '94. All concerned had gathered to witness and celebrate the signing of the contract. To get to this point, the band had been working for seven years, so when someone tells you that there's no such thing as an overnight sensation, I can testify that it's true.

It also heralded my first official day at the EG Music Group as I was 'on the job', and for this now 26-year-old, it marked nearly 11 years from leaving school to get to the exact point I wanted to get to. The call to my long-suffering parents was sweet. Finally, their son had a 'proper job' in the music industry.

The band joined a long list of illustrious artists that'd been part of the EG stable. Roxy Music, Brian Ferry, Emerson Lake and Palmer, King Crimson, Robert Fripp, Brian Eno, and still on the current roster, renowned industrial post-punk band, Killing Joke.

I met them during my first week on the job.

"Harvey, I'm Geordie from Killing Joke, how're you doing, man?" Geordie Walker greeted me with a smile.

Articulate and suave in a dystopian old English manner, I liked Geordie immediately, and he made time for me when we met.

Killing Joke were incredibly unique and not easy to handle, that was for sure.

Lead singer Jazz Coleman was especially intense, and I would often overhear disagreements with the EG management that would sometimes cause chaos in the office. Although I still chuckle to myself about the handwritten fax he sent me just after I joined EG, it read:

"Harvey, DO NOT FAIL. Jaz."

In 1994, Killing Joke had two separate entries in the official UK singles chart. Millennium and the title track of their new album, Pandemonium. I urge you to search online for videos of the band performing these songs on BBC's Top of the Pops, the UK's longest-running and most popular music TV show. Then, you'll be in the same time frame and place I'm writing about now.

The band invited me to see them play a sold-out show at the Shepherds Bush Empire. The gig was electric, 2,000 fans could feel lightning pulsing through their bodies. I got to go backstage, an experience I'll never forget. They *lived* in an alternative reality.

The dressing room had been 'redecorated' into some Moroccan kaftan tent. All the furniture had been replaced with heavily woven rugs, drapes, and cushions. But that aside, the lasting memory was one of the smells of something not entirely legal and all the 'interesting' people attracted by it. It was an actual den of iniquity.

I had to drag myself to the EG office the next day, I was shattered, but I didn't want to miss a second. I shared an office with Chris Kettle, an EG man, through and through. He was Sam's trusty lieutenant who'd been there for years and seen almost everything there was to see.

He was my mentor, and we'd become well acquainted as we shared an office. Our objective was to get a big record label to take the band's recording and marketing commitments on, with EG playing the role they always did as a production company.

We were going to get the band to release one single to see what kind of reaction they'd get from the industry now that EG were officially on board.

Smalltown Heroes were effectively wholly unknown and would, under normal circumstances, face an uphill battle to break through. But these weren't regular times. It was 1994/5, and we were in the middle of the 'Brit Pop' phenomenon.

'Brit Pop' was a British-based music genre and culture movement that emphasised Britishness. It produced catchier alternative rock, and you'll know some of the bands featured as part of this scene. Oasis is the most well-known one for most people. Smalltown Heroes *could* fit into this genre despite being a little more classic and international sounding, but we needed something extra to get them noticed.

"I've got an idea," said Sam with a twinkle in his eye. "A ground-breaking idea."

"You have? What is it?" I stopped what I was doing.

"We're going to release the first interactive single. Ever. By anyone."

It turned out he had a vested business interest in a two-man start-up that pioneered multi-media discs, something that hadn't been done commercially before.

It was the era of the CD-ROM taking over from the floppy disc. Computer magazines ran towards the new shiny discs like they were winning lottery tickets, putting them on their cover mounts at every opportunity. And it was no surprise either if you consider that at the time, my copy of Microsoft Office was on 26 floppy discs. Welcome to computing early 90s style.

This created a distribution opportunity as the computer magazines had the format and distribution but, critically, not enough content, given their nascency.

Sam's idea was brilliant. Put music, video, photos, and information about the band together on one disc. A single. The idea was a brilliant icebreaker for the band and an introduction to their music on the back of a technology shift!

All the content existed except a video, so we got a video for the lead song 'Moral Judgement' shot on a budget at the most diminutive budget-friendly studio you could think of. Pinewood Studios. If you've never heard of Pinewood, this is where the James Bond sound stage is and where huge movies have been shot for over eighty years, from Chitty Chitty Bang Bang to Jurassic World.

The biggest challenge was that there was no precedent on how to do it. Plus, managing the perception of an industry that could not decide if it was a music single or a computer disc was a delicate balancing act.

For example, one of the biggest music retailers placed it in their PC aisle at the time, not in the music section where it should've been. But, despite solvable problems, it did meet its objective of raising the band's profile.

Amongst other notable achievements, it got featured in weekly rock bible Kerrang! as 'Single of the Week', a VH1/MTV feature interview with the band and the highly viewed Saturday morning TV show, 'Music Games and Videos', which played the video and did an interview with lead singer, Chris. And...er...me!

There were also some missteps and poor choices. When leading broadcaster Sky asked the band to come on a Saturday morning TV show, we jumped at it. I failed to ask enough questions in advance, and the band ended up having to dress up like druids and play along with a kid's narrative that was far from representing them accurately. It was *so* cringeworthy.

One unforgettable moment was when we showed up at a theme park to play a show to find that the 'stage' was in some sort of Charlie and the Chocolate Factory Umpa Lumpa land. It was the only gig we ever walked out of before unpacking the van!

At this stage of the band's development, we'd have attended the opening of an envelope if we'd been asked.

The days were very long, but the band didn't complain because it felt like everything was working out. They worked very hard but also had fun when and where they could.

On just one night on tour, I observed ritual fart lighting (and burnt pubes), road crew pissing down the back of a TV (whilst it was on) and framed reproduction prints being taken off a hotel's wall and disturbing messages and pictures drawn on the back of them (and then rehung). I wonder if anyone ever noticed?

When I got back to London, Sam called me into his office. I wondered if we'd got a bill from the hotel. A pissed-on TV would not be cheap to replace.

"Hey, Harvey..."

"I'd like you to attend the Popkomm Music Industry Conference in Cologne, Germany. I reckon you're ready for it...."

Phew!

I walked through the conference doors a few days later, feeling energised. I had a healthy folder of impressive-looking press and media clips and was ready to network as I'd never networked before.

I headed to the big red double-decker London bus that dominated the internal skyline of the conference floor. Peter Knight was there too, and he helped out with some introductions.

"Harvey, I'd like you to meet Sue."

"Hi, nice to meet you," I said with unusual confidence.

"You too," she giggled back.

This one introduction rocked my world in more ways than one.

Alberts Music Publishing was the Australian-based company behind AC/DC, and Peter had just introduced me to their UK office representative. She was very friendly and bubbly, making my usual slightly uncomfortable manner around women I liked disappear. So much so that I found myself uttering the unexpected words, "Dinner tonight?"

To my amazement, she accepted!

Dinner was more of a friendly, cordial business affair, but as we talked, we found out we lived just three streets away from each other in London.

OK, yes, we hooked up and ended up living together.

During the three years or so that we were together, I had no intention of getting involved with AC/DC. They were my childhood heroes, and I wasn't going to put my then-girlfriend, who effectively worked for them, in a difficult position.

Until one day, she phoned me.

"Harv, I've got Angus and Malcolm here (AC/DC guitarists), and George (Young, their brother and producer). They're asking me if I know anyone with an original copy of AC/DC – *Live From The Atlantic Studios*," she asked me with a tone of slight desperation and little hope.

"Why are they asking that?" I quizzed.

"Because [pause] they are working in the recording studio here on a Bon Scott boxset of rarities. They are digitising some of the most popular unreleased recordings, one of which is *Atlantic*."

This was mind-blowing news to me. The *Atlantic* album was one of the band's most significant rarities. Never released, only ever in existence as a promo-only album in 1977. Very few copies were manufactured, and they were not in general circulation. A genuine copy could cost you £200-300 if you could even find one.

"George has the original analogue master tapes here, but at the start of the first song, the old tape is corrupted, and he can't recover it. The band don't keep their rare recordings, so none of them has a hard copy. By any stretch of possibility, do you have one or know where to get one in the fan community?" my girlfriend asked as if she felt like she was wasting her breath even asking.

"Yeah, I have TWO copies!" I said reassuringly.

"Harv! You are an angel! Can we borrow them?" she squealed.

"Of course!" I felt elated. The 12" vinyl was sitting 8 feet away from me on a shelf. She had thought the solution to the puzzle was so distant, yet she had no idea how close the answer was.

The next day, the album went to the Alberts studio with Sue. She carried it as if it were nitro-glycerine. A few hours later, she called.

"George wanted to say thank you to you; he recorded the part he needed off your original vinyl copy and dubbed it onto the beginning of the recording," she said.

The project had been saved. *Live from The Atlantic Studios* was included in AC/DC's *Bonfire* box set. It's even officially documented in the liner notes of the CD, it just doesn't tell the whole story or mention me by name. AC/DC guitarist Malcolm Young sent me a box set personally signed with his thanks. I still have it to this day.

My childhood obsession and AC/DC nerdiness had helped the band. And little did I know that my involvement with AC/DC would continue for a few years.

Back at my day job at EG, despite some progress in raising the band's profile, we had very little interest from record labels and had to consider the next move.

At the In the City music trade conference in Manchester,

Peter and I somehow managed to convince his (German) boss, Peter Kirsten, to commit to recording an album. We were hoping that the quality and anticipated increased exposure would garner the required industry interest.

The plan was that EG would release it in the UK and Global, via their licencing arrangement with the major heavyweight label, BMG Ariola, would release it in Germany.

But who would produce the album?

This is usually a creative decision, but for a band like Smalltown Heroes, every opportunity to drive their credibility had to be taken.

"Harv, I want a big-name producer on this. It's going to help the industry story immeasurably," Sam proclaimed.

I didn't necessarily disagree, but the band wanted Bird & Bush. Creatively they were proven to be a great fit. Even though this *should've* been a creative argument from Sam's point of view, it was a commercial one.

"I want an album that's going to push everything forward exponentially. A big name on an unknown band's record will be our sledgehammer to open doors."

We were on a tight budget, so a big-name producer would have to work to near-pro-bono levels. If I were to find such a person, they'd have to *love* the band. Because they'd be paid in love first and hope that money (royalties) would come later.

So, I had to find a big-name producer and get him to fall in love with the band. Sounds easy, right?

After Sam had got his little black book out (I kid you not, he had a little black book of key industry contacts) and I made a few phone calls, the door that seemed to open the widest was Chris Kimsey's.

Chris is most famous for co-producing The Rolling Stones' *Undercover* and *Steel Wheels* albums, but his credits as a producer, engineer, or mixer with and outside of The Rolling Stones are near-endless.

We could use Chris's credibility with The Rolling Stones to tell a story around the Smalltown Heroes.

Chris liked the band but decided it would be limited to just two songs if he were to be involved. Pro-bono has its limits, and so did our budget. This left a hole in our plan, though, two tracks on an album produced by Chris, the rest by whom?

Marshall Bird and Steve Bush had been with the band along this long journey and were in it to win it. They too were looking for a break as producers, having never had any of their work commercially released at this level before.

They were a safe pair of hands, and we knew what we'd get. Anyone else would be a sojourn into the unknown, and in the end, despite no one liking the outcome, it was decided that Bird & Bush would produce the album, bar two tracks. Chris Kimsey would produce two tracks of *his* choice.

We invested in what we knew and who had supported us along the way with this album. Battery Studios would be where most of the album would be recorded and mixed, and Bird & Bush would produce.

The 'special sauce' would come from two tracks produced by Chris Kimsey, recorded and mixed at Metropolis Studios.

When it came to mastering the album, Steve Bush and I flew to New York to witness Ted Jensen at Sterling Sound sprinkling his magic on compiling the final product. This was a walk in dreamland for me as I knew he'd mastered the classic AC/DC album, *Back in Black*.

He was cordial enough for me to ask him questions about AC/DC, and he offered a few horror stories of his own about other bands. I quickly learnt that no matter how successful you become, the problems don't disappear; they get bigger!

Whilst work on the album was ongoing, I set about the launch plan, which very much focused on exposing the band to as many people in a concert setting as possible.

In short, they had to find an audience, and the best way to do that was to go out on the road in support of a name (established) band, opening up the bill.

The competition to open for a name band is fierce. I had my feelers out big time. I called every agent and every promoter of note. And after numerous false dawns with other name bands, I came across one opportunity that might just work.

The Jeff Healey Band were a Canadian blues rock band best known for performing the soundtrack for 'Roadhouse,' a movie starring actor Patrick Swayze.

They had their most tremendous success in the late 1980s, when the band recorded the album *See the Light*. It reached platinum status in the United States by selling more than one million copies and selling two million copies worldwide.

Jeff Healey himself was blind and sat on stage with his guitar across his lap. Despite this, it didn't hamper his incredible playing whatsoever.

I had connected with his agent in London two years previously, as he had been one of the three companies to respond to my faxes. So, the Smalltown Heroes and the progress they'd made were well known to him as we'd always kept in touch.

In those days, it was not uncommon for prospective support bands to be asked for a 'buy-on.'

Tom Stephen, the drummer from The Jeff Healey Band, who was band leader, cordially agreed to Smalltown Heroes being the only support on their up-and-coming UK tour. But we had to grease the wheels to make it happen.

I made the case to Sam (EG) and Peter (Global) that the visibility from this tour would be a crucial stepping stone to help album sales. They cut a cheque for the buy-on. But the logistics cost way more if you consider a tour bus cost £550 per day, and keeping a band and crew watered, fed and paid was on top.

But, with special guest status negotiated for the Smalltown Heroes, their name appeared on all the key promotional communication for the tour. It was a significant step up, especially if you saw some of the venues' profiles. No clubs this time but 2,000-3,000 seat theatres.

I did the whole of this tour as Tour Manager as well. Not only to save costs, but as it was the lads' first major tour, I wanted to savour the occasion. We'd all been in this together for *years,* and stepping aboard the big tour bus with two lounges, bunk beds, a kitchen, WC, and our dedicated driver was incredible.

The tour was a huge success in terms of the response to the band. They won over crowds in most of the places they went, but three shows stood out for me.

Manchester Apollo was the show I'd been looking forward to the most. I'd spent my entire teenage years watching heavy rock bands there, and my first-ever gig was there. On 3rd October 1982, I saw AC/DC in concert on the *For Those About to Rock* tour. Thirteen years later, I was there with the band I discovered and managed.

This was some sort of personal karma moment.

The other two shows that stood out were at the Cambridge Corn Exchange and London's Shepherds Bush Empire. For the simple reason that when the band went on, the house was full, unusual for a support band, and the Smalltown Heroes played off the energy of a large audience and took the roof off.

They could have had an encore. Unheard of for most support bands.

Fortunately, all the band's industry team were at the Shepherds Bush show, and it reminded them why they kept writing the cheques and what potential they had in their hands.

Unfortunately, none of the other music industry folks we invited showed up.

Soon after the tour, we reconvened and prepared to release the band's second single, 'Spin.'

Money to invest was tight, though, and the business case conversations were more difficult, especially at EG. The reality was that, despite ongoing progress, two key things had not materialised:

1. No one else in the music industry showed much interest in the band, and
2. Critical acclaim did not convert to sales (so far).

The model we were pursuing was the age-old one on which EG had built its previous success. Use other people's money, keep all the intellectual property to yourself and when you have a successful artist like Roxy Music, you have leverage for the other artists.

Since they sold their intellectual property to Richard Branson's Virgin Records and media giant Bertelsmann, they didn't have that artist profile anymore. They were starting over.

'Spin' was one of the songs Chris Kimsey produced. Initially, it didn't have a video shot because no one wanted to pay for it, despite us being in the golden MTV era. The record pluggers objected, stating that the single would be doomed without a video. So, I scraped £3,000 to get a single camera shoot done.

Even with a video, the single bombed. It sank without a trace. We faced a long, hard slog.

The album, titled *Human Soup,* was finished. I got the band on another tour in the UK to get the band in front of more people. This time the tour was with The Stranglers. Another buy-on.

Baz and Tony from Smalltown Heroes were massive fans of The Stranglers, a band they looked up to as heroes and mentors. But elsewhere, there were misgivings about whether it was a good fit. Would this be the right target audience for the band?

KEY LESSONS IN LIFE AND BUSINESS

REPUTATION DOESN'T ALWAYS MEAN YOU'LL BE HAPPY WITH THE RESULTS

Reputation alone is not enough. To have real equity, the work must be great or better than you might've usually expected. After all, a reputation comes from being earned.

Chris Kimsey was a big name, and I can't deny that we didn't milk it for everything it was worth. However, in the studio, it very quickly became evident that what he'd produce would be wildly different from what we expected.

In one case at Metropolis Studios, he used a lot of Bird & Bush's backing vocal recordings of the band in his two tracks because he said he couldn't do it better and it would save time. Steve and Marshall did great work but suffered because, through no fault of their own, they had no reputation at this point, and we needed leverage for the band wherever we could get it.

So, after being 'relegated' to doing 80% of the album, 'awkward' doesn't go any way to describe how I felt when I had to phone them to ask if Chris Kimsey could use *their* work to save time and effort.

The band *wanted* to like what he did because he was a nice guy and because of his reputation.

But they didn't. And neither did I.

CONTEXT MATTERS (AGAIN)

When I worked for EG in London, I did the same work I'd done in Sunderland a few years earlier. But it yielded different results because the context was different. I'd repositioned myself as a credible manager, despite the unknown band I was responsible for.

I wasn't sitting in a dirty flat, struggling to pay the bills. I represented a well-known successful music company. And therefore, I was a credible music manager by definition.

People underestimate the importance of context, but it's probably one of the essential things in life and business. It serves as a critical mental shortcut so that people can quickly decide whether they should care about something or not.

CHAPTER 16

SHOT DOWN IN FLAMES

"**N**o shitting in the toilet, lads," said the tour bus driver. "I don't have many rules, but there's no way I'm emptying the septic tank with 'solids' in it whilst driving you around Europe. I don't get paid enough."

"Understood," I replied, speaking for the band too. They were too busy having a crack and opening cans of beer to celebrate the first day of a new tour.

We'd played some tour dates in the UK, but with the album released in Germany too, we'd booked some European shows, opening for The Stranglers. Smalltown Heroes were going international!

Playing France, Germany, and the Netherlands was in some ways, a step up, and it would certainly be interesting to see how audiences from other countries would respond to the band. It felt good to be doing it right; on the nights when the audience for us was thin, it was a sobering reminder of how far we had to go and how hard and expensive it would be.

In the middle of the night after the Amsterdam show, as we approached the border between the Netherlands and Germany, the toilet rule was sternly put to the test. Lead singer Chris was more than desperate, and after much whining, the driver stopped the bus so he could find somewhere in the woods 'to go.'

In the pitch black, from the deepest ether, we heard a faint and distant voice... "I'm all right, lads, I've found a spot," Chris shouted, his torch a mere flicker in the woods.

Only we weren't on the bus anymore!

A small group of us got out. We'd walked around and to the back of Chris in a pincer movement, one group to the left, one to the right. Once behind Chris, we'd turned our torches on and, like a pack of rabid wolves, started running towards Chris, shouting and randomly waving the torches around in the trees.

The poor guy thought there was some sort of alien invasion because, scared out of his wits, he started to run through the woods towards the bus with his pants still down and some 'unfinished business' on a large leaf!

"Whoooaaa lads, lads, I'm being chased, help me! It's going to kill me, heeeellllllppp meeeeee!"

It was only when he got to the side of the bus, panting heavily and almost in tears, that he realised that it wasn't an alien invasion, but rather his bandmates chasing him for fun.

"You fucking bastards!" Chris knew he had well and truly been had. The funniest part was watching it back on the video we'd shot. The shaky video was like an amateur horror B-movie and took the hilarity of the moment to a whole new level. Much crack ensued that night as we continued our night drive through Germany, all to Chris's obvious displeasure.

Despite the jolly japery on the road, no external labels were knocking at our door. After a very serious conversation with Peter Kirsten, the founder and owner of Global Music, we decided to focus on the deal that we *did* have.

Global Records had a blanket licencing deal with media giant BMG, who owned RCA, Ariola, Arista, and other notable record labels. Under the terms of the agreement, BMG *had* to release the Smalltown Heroes album. But only in Germany.

The goal was to see if, with this connection, we could leverage it beyond Germany. If the band had sold any decent number of records to date, this wouldn't have been the hardest challenge; however, there were no notable sales to evangelise.

If there had been, I'd have been instigating a bidding war from record labels everywhere.

So, the BMG Worldwide charm offensive began in earnest. I talked my way into the London office on more than one occasion, and I met BMG in Japan, but the highest-powered meeting was in New York.

I targeted Rudi Gassner. He was one of BMG Entertainment's most prominent international executives and was known for his ability to take a local act from another country and give them international appeal. He was also a close contact of Peter Kirsten at Global Music.

I knew there was no way I could cold-call him, so I devised a plan. I'd ask Peter Kirsten to call him first to warm him up, add credibility and say I'd be calling.

A few days later, I called Rudi Gassner at his office in New York and got through the first time. I couldn't believe it. I was talking to one of *the* top record executives in the world. Not just at BMG but at *any* record label.

"Ya, hello Harvey, how are you?" he cordially greeted me.

"Good morning Mr. Gassner, very well, and thank you for taking my call," I said with confidence that defied the band's actual status.

"Peter Kirsten said you'd be calling, how can I help you?" he said.

In reality, this call was like using a sledgehammer to crack a walnut, but the call's outcome was clear. Come to New York, tell us the story, play us some music, and we'll take it from there.

I knew I wasn't meeting Rudi Gassner; I was meeting an A&R guy who had been delegated this meeting by him. Frankly, without sales figures, as we sat in his office in Times Square, talking and then listening to the band, he didn't seem to care much. He was going through the motions.

It was a long flight back, and consumed with the feeling of emptiness, I started to question myself. What was I doing wrong?

Back in London and after trying again to pitch the band to our licenced label, BMG, things were looking increasingly desperate as the doors shut in my face at every turn.

Were we going to have to do everything, literally everything ourselves? What was the point of record labels if they showed no creative interest?

London Music Week was a new industry festival of gigs and events that was being publicised, and somehow, I managed to get the Smalltown Heroes a headline gig at the well-known Borderline Club in the centre of London.

If they won't come to us, I thought, I'll have to get the band in front of them when I know industry folks will be swarming venues in London.

This was a first, we had a support band – an unknown (to us) three-piece band from Wales.

They were called Stereophonics.

The gig was packed to the rafters, sweat dripping off the ceiling, and I thought nothing of the Stereophonics, to be honest. They were good, frontman Kelly wore a shaggy Afghan jacket that made him look like a wolf, but other than that, they weren't remarkable.

What *was* remarkable was that Richard Branson's new label, V2, was there, as were Bird & Bush, who were there to see Smalltown Heroes. Of course.

Probably realising that their album with the Smalltown

Heroes wasn't setting the world alight, Bird & Bush offered the Stereophonics some free studio time to do demos.

And it was these demos and the fact that the 'Phonics started becoming the latest darlings of the trendy music press that saw them sign a recording contract with V2 Records.

Oi!

Steve Bush and Marshall Bird had approached Stereophonics in the same way they'd done with my lads, but even at this point, their success was far from guaranteed. The deliberation from V2 records as to whether they should produce the 'Phonics album at all seemed to rumble on for quite some time.

Regardless, it was none of my business. Only it was! The Stereophonics got signed from my show, not the Smalltown Heroes!

What the hell was it going to take to get the industry onside? I'd seen thousands and thousands of people love the band live, but since the 'World's First Interactive Single,' we were getting no national media exposure whatsoever.

We were picking up industry supporters along the way, though. Most people who saw the band play live got what I got. And for a change, I got a call from a promoter in Hamburg, Germany, with a proposition.

"Hi Harvey, thanks for taking my call. I saw the band supporting The Stranglers, and I loved them," he said. "I wanted to know if they would like to tour Germany with Stoppok?" said Michael Bisping from A.S.S. Concerts.

"Urm…" I had no idea who Stoppok were. "That sounds real… good," I said, "I'm sure the lads would love to. Could you send me the dates, and I'll confirm in the next couple of days?"

As soon as the call ended, I quickly did an internet search and discovered that Stoppok was a very popular German rock musician. He would be a much better fit with a younger audience than The Stranglers had.

To be invited and not be asked for a buy-on was refreshing. But the reality was that we were running out of money.

Sam was dodging callers at the office chasing payment, and I was getting my salary deferred. I didn't get paid for two months, and that bit me, yet Sam reassured me I'd get paid. To be fair, I did, eventually, after having to live off a bank loan.

Something bigger was happening at EG than the lack of commercial progress for the band. I couldn't fathom it out entirely, though, no one could. On the surface, everything was as it was. Glossy Chelsea office and all the same aspirations. But changes started to be very noticeable.

The calls for payment became more frequent. Some vendors wouldn't work with us because we'd not paid them for six months. We weren't talking large sums of money here either, sometimes just a few hundred pounds.

Accounts were on hold, and I had to start dodging calls. If you happen to know me, that's just not me. I shoot straight dice and run a tidy ship. But this wasn't my ship.

Sam had many interests, the music company being one and his farm being another. But what was clear was that no one understood the complexity or opaqueness of Sam's financial situation.

What we *did* know was that Sam was struggling with the fallout of the Lloyds Names being called upon to cover unprecedented liabilities in the insurance market.

The band's monthly retainers, a set of cheques I'd send from EG each month for the band to live off, started getting later and later. I'd get irate calls from band members worried they'd be unable to pay their rent or utility bills.

Money was *that* tight.

So, when an opportunity came in to play in Germany on a sold-out tour, it was more than a difficult sell.

"No," said Sam, "get our friends at Global Music in Germany

to pay for it." And somehow, Peter and I managed it, and the tour went ahead.

But everything was different. The budget was slashed, so there were fewer personnel on the road, and the tour bus had to go. The band had to go back to a van and stay in motels.

Even I didn't go on this tour. One less mouth to feed and one less motel room to pay for. And to be honest, I didn't want to go.

Reports from the tour, however, were exemplary. The band were pleasing and entertaining crowds, so I did fly out for one show.

The tour's last date was in Munich, the city where not just Global Music was based but BMG too. All of BMG was invited to come to see Smalltown Heroes play as we were in their backyard.

The folks from Global came, including the boss, Peter Kirsten, but it soon became apparent that no one from BMG locally went to the show. It was like they couldn't care less. The cold hard reality was that even though they *had* to put the band's album out, they didn't *want* to.

Regardless, we all partied hard that night. I had a 7am flight back to London, so I stayed up all night chain-smoking cigarettes, drinking beers, and generally destroying myself with the band.

By 5am, I was in a vassal-like state. I couldn't breathe. As I lay on the club floor, it was like someone had put an elephant on my chest.

I was the lucky one. The band had to drive nearly 1,000 miles to get home with a hangover from hell. As I entered the airport, I threw a near-full pack of Marlboro Lights in the trash.

I never smoked again.

The cycle of this album had run its course. Even with more money, there was nothing more that could have been done that hadn't already been done. A super-human effort had, in effect, yielded... nothing tangible.

I had one final idea. Maybe fresh material would provide a fresh impetus? We headed North.

We were in a studio in Newcastle, just getting some ideas down, when a call came in. Tom Jones wanted *that* studio on *that* particular day.

The Tom Jones.

"Tom can have the studio right now," I said to his manager Mark (who is also his son) "if the band can have a photo with Tom and we can use it for publicity."

"That's fine by me. Let's do it," Mark responded. That photo was worth more in press interest than the cost of the studio!

A few weeks later, I was playing some of the demos back in the EG office, and nothing particularly stood out until...

"Whoooaaaa, what the hell is this song?" I loudly asked no one in particular. I played it again.

"Whoooaaaa," I played it again. And again, and again.

Sam came out of his office after hearing some of my self-generated commotions.

"What's that, Harv?" he enquired with a new-found enthusiasm.

"It's from the new Smalltown Heroes demos," I proudly announced.

"It's a fucking hit record, is what that is," he declared as his business twinkle started to appear.

"That's our ticket," he went on, "We have to release it!"

Woo-hoo! Who was I to disagree? It *was* a hit record. But for someone else!

'Go Your Own Way' was a signature song for Fleetwood Mac from their famous 1977 album, *Rumours*, and for reasons I'm still not sure of, the Smalltown Heroes decided to record it without telling anyone.

Maybe they thought nothing of it when they recorded it. They certainly didn't expect my phone call to tell them it would be released on EG Records as a single.

Maybe that was the icebreaker we needed for the national media to finally give the band some love. It wasn't unheard of for a band to break out with a cover song, after all.

The reality of the band's predicament was more acute than they knew at the time. Their contract with EG would soon come to its full term of three years, and it was far from guaranteed that it would be renewed.

But regardless, we got the song remixed by Steve Bush and released it. With no video.

The phone started to ring for TV appearances, the biggest of which was a prime-time TV chat show in Ireland. A fresh take on a classic song had sparked *some* interest, but critically, there was *still* no national radio play.

I thought maybe the TV we did and the press we got would get us the sales and recognition we needed to kick on, but sadly, it wasn't to be.

The single did chart. It peaked at #104 on the official UK singles chart. Hardly a euphoric achievement.

The band seemed to believe that everything would just continue as it was. The monthly retainer would keep showing up, the studio sessions, the tours, there was always something next, always more to do.

But, the financial situation at EG was getting worse. The contract period was coming close, but Sam's creditors and lifestyle were in closer focus.

Throughout these years, EG had very little income. They'd sold all of their legacy catalogues for millions with Sam's original partner at EG, Mark Fenwick, bowing out of EG but not the industry. Even while I was there, Mark managed Pink Floyd bassist Roger Waters.

Sam carried the EG torch himself for the first time and aspired to revisit past glories with new ones. Only his lifestyle hadn't changed. On the surface, life seemed to go on as if Roxy Music were still bashing out the hits and the magic money tree would continue to yield lots of cash.

Even *if* the Smalltown Heroes had achieved everything they set out to, the commission wouldn't have covered much of the outgoings. And Killing Joke's sold-out shows and two hit singles didn't make a dint either.

The highly polished veneer started to show cracks. Sam's Smith Street three-story townhouse in Chelsea was the first to go as he and his family moved to the farm they owned on the Isle of Man.

The Isle of where? The Isle of Man is a tiny self-governing island in the Irish Sea that's part of the British Crown but enjoys individual autonomy. It's known for its well-established finance and offshore tax sector.

Then, part of the office was sub-let, and the band's contract ran its course. It wasn't renewed.

"Baz, all right, mate? So, I have the news you've been waiting for on your contract," hesitant silence met my opening line on the phone.

"But it's not the news you want. EG isn't renewing your contract. I'm sorry."

I didn't need to wait long for the expected response. Mostly searing anger and words I can't reprint here, but in the end, understandable frustration and, once the reality of the retainers hit home, desperation.

"How are we going to live?" Baz batted back an obvious and anticipated concern.

I repeated the phone call with every member of the band. I'd dropped a bombshell on them, and it hurt so bad. For them and me.

I was given extra time to see if anything else would come up, like Black Sabbath unexpectedly walking through the door looking for new management! Failing this, I'd be leaving too.

The opportunity at EG had great potential, but the lack of investment, commercial success and diversity in the portfolio didn't match the aspiration.

Much to the Smalltown Heroes' chagrin, I *did* sign another band whilst at EG.

Honeycrack had had a top 40 album and two top 40 singles whilst signed with Epic Records (Sony) but had recently and unexpectedly left the label on the eve of a UK tour.

I got the band's next single, 'Anyway,' on EG Records as a one-off deal with an option for their next album. Without marketing spend or radio play (or internet), the song went to #67 on the UK charts. Yet, EG didn't exercise the option for the next album, and soon after, Honeycrack split up.

So, I left EG, too, with post-dated cheques for the remainder of my salary. Maybe I shouldn't have been surprised that one of them bounced.

Yet, the Smalltown Heroes were still signed to Global Music, who unexpectedly exercised the option to make a second album. To his massive credit, Peter Kirsten wanted to have another go at BMG, this time with new material.

The backdrop to all this was very different, however. The band had no retainer to live off. They had no formal management; the manager they had in me was unemployed and needed to get a salaried job.

I agreed to help the band with management representation on the understanding that I would have to look for paid work elsewhere. Effectively, I was working pro-bono.

The negotiations were different too. The band wanted to take on a heavier sound with their new material, and I got Global to agree to enlist Simon Efemey as Producer, best known for producing The Wildhearts' sonic assault of an album, *P.H.U.Q.*

A key defining factor to even getting the album recorded was that Global insisted on it being recorded in Munich, Germany, at their studio, ARCO. This was to save costs and keep the flow of money within the Global group of companies. It was also so Peter Kirsten could, understandably, keep a closer eye on what was going on.

The band shacked up in a serviced apartment for six weeks and got on with the recording. I flew over for a visit halfway through, and all seemed well enough, but I ran into a profound creative issue.

Global wanted their principal engineer at ARCO to mix the album to keep more control of the result and the costs in the company's circular economy. Fearing poor results, I humoured the suggestion and recommended he do a track, and we'd base the decision on the results.

Which, thankfully for my business case, were fucking shocking! So, Simon agreed to mix the album on the condition that it was done back in England at Jacobs Studios. At considerable expense.

And, with no other credible option, I managed to get Peter Kirsten to agree to pay for it.

Despite my uncertain future, I was still making things happen for the band, in the interest of the band.

I went to Jacobs Studios to hear the album come together in the mix, but the band wanted a formal sit-down meeting with me out of the blue.

"Harv, mate, you've been there for us through thick and thin, given us everything," said Baz.

"But you don't have the backing of EG or a big management company anymore, and we need a manager with influence, someone who can help us kick on," added Chris.

"We know you need to look for paid work," said Tony, as some sort of justification.

I listened carefully and said nothing. I scanned the room as the words hit my ears and were processed by my brain.

Kev, Smalltown Heroes drummer, looked in pain as he avoided my gaze.

"So, we've decided that Simon's manager, Rudy, will look after us from now on," finished Baz.

After nearly ten years of championing the cause, I was *fired*.

Maybe they expected me to lose my shit, but I just stood quietly and left. As I did, Kev ran out to talk to me. He didn't necessarily agree with the decision or how it had been done.

But it *was* done. And as I reflected on the train ride back home to London, *I* was done. This time, for good.

And despite being finished, the second album, titled *Atomic Café* was never released.

Within a year, the band folded. What would the future hold for me?

KEY LESSONS IN LIFE AND BUSINESS

PAST ACHIEVEMENTS ARE NO GUARANTEE OF FUTURE SUCCESS

I got fired after ten years of working with the band despite them finishing a second album. In purely commercial terms, they couldn't have expected to record it.

Despite the past achievements, thousands and thousands of people enjoying their shows against all odds, only one key performance indicator mattered. Sales. And the band didn't have anywhere near enough of them.

The opportunities and access I had to industry people would've yielded different results if they had. Because, no matter what the most creative of music biz people will tell you, they're all chasing the next big (sales) thing.

Past critical acclaim wasn't enough; in the end, we ran out of road. Literally and metaphorically.

THE LAW OF ATTRACTION

This law is pervasive in life as well as business. Simply put, like attracts like.

In the context of the band, all Brit-pop bands were getting signed with Stereophonics *just* about qualifying as they had a little more indie edge than our boys, and the independent music press loved them. Because Smalltown Heroes weren't Brit-pop, they had to cross a chasm and meet resistance every step of the way.

This law is immutable and without realising it, you always struggle with it. Give it some thought.

HAVING A GOOD PRODUCT IS NOT GOOD ENOUGH

Smalltown Heroes were a great rock and roll band with great melody and were a killer act on stage. They had all the vital ingredients: A good-looking and distinctive lead singer, an energetic and charismatic lead guitar player, and a tight solid rhythm section.

They entertained crowds and made outstanding records; anyone who witnessed them was left impressed.

But being *great* isn't good enough. Especially not in the 90s, as you were at the mercy of the cartels of major record labels and a narrow but influential media. Pre-internet, your options to reach an audience were *very* constrained.

I've always maintained that, together with a fashion for Brit-pop at the time, the band's sound was just too classic international rock at the time. Ironically, you may even say timeless.

If their albums were new in modern times, they could take their shot on the internet, and they'd likely do well enough.

The context has changed so much that I'm sure they'd find an audience.

But it's about thirty years too late.

SMALLTOWN HEROES

▲ Building relationships with Steve Bush and Marshall Bird (front middle) on an early session at Chipping Norton Recording Studios.

Smalltown Heroes   EG

◄ Investment money from EG starts to show its worth. Iconic photos of the band shot by rockstar photographer, Scarlet Page, daughter of Jimmy Page of Led Zeppelin fame.
(L-R. Tony Roffe, Baz Warne, Chris Warne, Kevin Scott)

BAZ WARNE + CHRIS WARNE OF Smalltown Heroes   EG

▼ Tom Jones with the band. Do I need to say more? Legend.

▼ The bigger the stage, the more impressive the band was.

▲ The video shoot for 'Spin.'

CHAPTER 17
WIND OF CHANGE

"I'll be alright, Mum. Don't worry," I said over the phone, trying to convince her and myself.

"Are you sure, Harvey? You've got your mortgage to pay?" she replied.

"I promise, Mum. I've got an interview next week. I feel good about it. I'll ring you back next Friday and let you know how I've got on." I ended the call and collapsed on my bed.

Being out of work for six months had been a massive kick in the nuts. I had two months left before I risked losing everything I'd built in the previous three years.

I'd been searching for a job non-stop, but the popularity of this new thing called 'the internet' was hitting the music industry hard. The advent of the MP3 music format saw new ways of sharing and distributing music. Critically for the music industry, without people paying for their music.

A year or two earlier, Music Week (the UK equivalent of Billboard) seemed to have plenty of jobs advertised. Now, in 1997, the back pages seemed bereft of opportunities.

I'd had a few interviews for crappy jobs, done some voluntary work for Honeycrack's manager, and hung out at Alberts Studio when invited, but nothing had come of any of it.

But I did have one interview for an exciting job.

ZTT Records was formed in 1983 by producer, musician and writer Trevor Horn, his wife and manager Jill Sinclair, and journalist Paul Morley. The label based itself in Horn's west London studio, and I went there to be interviewed by Jill for a Label Manager job.

This was more credible; it was heady compared to getting paid by bouncing cheques. Frankie Goes to Hollywood and Seal had all of their major hits with ZTT, but the thing that was on my radar was Jill Sinclair's reputation as a *formidable* businesswoman. All the accolades and awards were down to her hard work and sheer determination in a male-dominated music industry.

I was so eager that I arrived half an hour early for my interview, dressed in a three-piece pinstripe suit, my hair neatly cut short. I felt like everything was riding on this interview going well.

The receptionist told me to take a seat. I was feeling anxious and slightly nauseous. I couldn't stop thinking about all the music history that had been through the doors. Before Jill and Trevor took over the building, it belonged to Island Records founder Chris Blackwell and was known as Island Studios and Basing Street Studios.

The history of this studio was immeasurable. I wasn't usually impressed or flustered, but this place was the palace that housed musical royalty. You had to pause and take note if your passion was music. The fact that some of Led Zeppelin IV was recorded in the studio was the passport to infinite rock mortality. A chill ran down my spine.

It's the understatement of the century to say that I was in illustrious company. Madonna, The Eagles, Dire Straits, Emerson, Lake & Palmer, Rihanna, Paul McCartney, The Rolling Stones,

Genesis, Led Zeppelin, Queen, Bob Marley, and Roxy Music. They'd all recorded here.

A few minutes ticked by, and an assistant came to greet and escort me up to the offices. As I walked through the corridors, it was like I could feel the eyes of the late Freddie Mercury and Bob Marley upon me. I could feel their voices reverberating inside my head, saying...

"Go on, lad, you *can* get this job. *We believe in you.*"

I was introduced to Jill in a small, private meeting room away from the noise of the main open-plan office.

Jill, as expected, was *very* businesslike in her manner and how she presented herself.

Her hair was in a neat bob, and she wore a blouse that looked more like a man's shirt. And she was *very* attentive. There wasn't a word or mannerism that didn't go unnoticed; I think I was getting some sort of business X-ray, and I'm pretty sure that she decoded me in mere minutes.

But it was plainer sailing than I was expecting or had prepared for. We seemed to click and understand each other. I seemed to have the qualities she was looking for, and after 30-40 minutes or so, Jill told me that she'd like me to meet Trevor.

Trevor Horn. Husband, co-owner and world-famous producer. I'd done it! I got through to the second interview!

The most challenging part of the interview was that I'd been in quite a lot of abdominal pain from trapped wind, but I'd tried to style it out and not let it show. But, as the interview went on, the pain subsided, or I just mentally overcame it, so I could focus on the job interview at hand.

At the end of the interview, we stood up, smiled, and arms reached out to shake hands. I firmly took Jill's hand and shook it, giving it my best business-like kung-fu grip. But as the grip gently tightened, disaster struck...

We had perfect eye contact, and at the exact moment I

squeezed Jill's hand, I unexpectedly squeezed out the loudest trumpet fart you've ever heard.

PAAAAAAARRRPPPPPPPPPPP!

It was like I'd repositioned myself from being a Label Manager into a walking whoopee cushion in front of one of the industry's most influential people.

Jeez! How do I react to this? Fall on my sword and say sorry or pretend it never happened? I think anyone within 30 metres knew it had happened.

I had mere milliseconds to decide. I chose the latter. I'm not even sure *she* knew how to react. The tiniest of wry smiles was the only visible acknowledgement she gave me, and we never spoke of it. Ever.

Indeed, I thought I'd undone *any* chance of an interview with Trevor Horn. In sports, this was like losing a game in the last seconds from a winning position.

I was left to let myself out, and as I walked back down the corridor, I could feel the ghostly presence of Freddie Mercury and Bob Marley tut-tutting and shaking their heads as I did the walk of shame towards the front door.

The full impact of what'd just happened hit me as I returned home. Not only would I have blown the best opportunity, but I also had nothing else on the horizon.

And then, like scoring an unexpected equaliser in the last seconds of a game, we went to extra time. The phone rang.

"Hello, is that Harvey?" said a cultivated media-type voice.

"Yes, it is," I said, trying to sound upbeat.

"It's Zara at ZTT Records. I'm phoning to set a date for you to come to see Trevor [Horn]. How are you fixed for next week?"

That's it, I'd forced the game into extra time! The crowd goes wild. I go wild. By myself, in my flat. How the hell did that happen? I farted in the presence of the critical decision-maker and still got the second interview.

So, a week later, I was back at ZTT and feeling confident that lightning, or farts, don't strike twice. I walked towards the same room that'd been the scene of the previous week's crime and could see Trevor Horn sitting there, waiting for me.

"Hi, Harvey. Thanks for coming in. Sorry I'm eating... bit of a crazy day," he said, not making eye contact.

"No worries," I replied. He had a plate of beans and toast on his knee, so he didn't get up.

"Tell me about yourself," as he gestured with his fork for me to take a seat.

I talked, he ate, and then the interview was over.

I've been out of work for six months, and things at home were getting frayed. The early optimism was slowly waning, the bills mounting and the outlook not so good. Damn them, MP3s!

After eight months, I was desperate. My girlfriend and I had set about preparing for doomsday. Selling the apartment and moving in together, and consolidating everything.

Then, from all my efforts, an interview came out of the blue, outside of London. One hundred and sixty-eight miles out of London, to be precise.

At this point, I thought, "what the heck." I borrowed my girlfriend's car, went to the interview and thought nothing else of it. Jokingly, I told Sue, "Ha-ha, I bet you I get this job!"

I did. Now I had my own conflict.

It was officially the start of my career re-launch – a new category to gain experience in and a new role as a Product Marketer.

Product marketing is a niche role within marketing, working across the whole organisation as the leading voice of the market and customer. Still, it's closest to the intersection of the product and marketing teams.

People use descriptions like 'you're the choreographer, not the dancer' or 'we're here not to do the work, but ensure the right work gets done.' Whatever analogy you pick, my music business background was perfect as I was used to leading the charge, driving change, working across multiple stakeholders, and spinning lots of plates simultaneously. The company that wanted to hire me recognised this and made me an offer.

As it's a niche, it was hard to hire product marketers. It still is today.

It was also *unofficially* the end of my relationship with my music business girlfriend and my time in the music business as I knew it.

We agreed that I'd do this job by living in the North of England five days a week and coming home to London for the weekends. I'd do this for at least six months, then look to get a job back in London so life could resume.

But my girlfriend threw me an almighty curveball on the *very* first day. I got an "I can't do this" and a wailing phone call, which was the beginning of the end. It was just a matter of time. The first weekend back in London was awful, the following more horrible, and after a month, I heard...

"You don't have to keep coming back, you know," and a few months later, we broke up.

Emotionally, this all played very heavily on me at the office, and occasionally, the emotional rollercoaster would visibly get the better of me.

The company I worked for, Gremlin Interactive, was seemingly on the up. A well-known independent game producer and publisher that had just IPO'ed. Great time to join! *Not.*

Being independently owned means the owners make the decisions. If you have cash flow, you have control. After an IPO, you're slaves to the shareholders and must meet *their* expectations.

To call it out, *you*, as the leadership team, set the shareholder's expectations.

But in this company, something was wildly off. Within the first quarter after floating, the company's results seemed to be at odds with the shareholder expectations. The anticipation of enormous sales for a new Nintendo game called Body Harvest was just that, internal anticipation. It felt like they bet the farm on hyping it, and much was lost on the back of poor sales.

The atmosphere in the place changed. Very quickly.

The reality was that they wanted to play with the big boys by becoming one of them but did not have the heavyweight ammunition to do so.

The internal culture and ongoing shenanigans didn't help either.

One staffer found solace with the office hottie, doing very describable things in indescribable places.

Another staffer, *the* most wholesome apple-pie Northern good girl, turned out to be the opposite. Her engagement with her childhood sweetheart was offset by the backdrop of her shagging *everyone* and *everything* in the office.

Except me. How the hell did I miss that? I only found out when the wedding was called off, and she went into therapy.

I tried to crack on with product positioning, localisation plans, and understanding why anyone would be playing games like Wild Metal Country or Tanktics.

Then one of the Directors made a desk move on our floor. The result was that all eligible women were now sitting next to, or opposite him. It was like he forged his own harem of girls! Maybe it's no surprise that a sexual harassment case came up quite quickly, as did his exit from the company.

But worst of all was the bitter, vindictive, and toxic atmosphere peddled by some individuals that permeated everywhere.

After less than six months of this, the company was seemingly on its knees and was looking for a suitor, which was a real shame because the potential had been huge.

In 1997, Gremlin Interactive had themselves acquired DMA Design, creators of Grand Theft Auto (GTA) and Lemmings.

GTA had already become a big hit, and there was some talk that I would be the Product Marketing Manager for GTA2, a game that would go on to be awarded Platinum sales status in the UK for its PlayStation release.

Unfortunately, it wasn't to be because Gremlin's financial issues were becoming too overbearing to ignore.

With ownership of DMA Design and a successful sports series in the portfolio, Gremlin looked like a bargain acquisition at the time.

Enter Infogrames, a powerhouse French Publisher with global reach. Their growth in the '90s came mainly from an aggressive acquisition strategy, and we got hoovered up for just over £20 million.

Ian Stewart, the founder and Managing Director of Gremlin, was a straight shooter. He always levelled with the staff and was very approachable. But, despite Ian planning to play a crucial part in the merger, an unexpected health issue determined that he wouldn't.

By the time Ian returned, he had found a very different company. It wasn't a merger but an inharmonious takeover.

I witnessed Bruno Bonnel, the enigmatic Infogrames CEO, conduct an all-hands meeting with the whole company. Promises of job security and a world of opportunity were made.

"The sky is blue; go as high as you want!" he said at a company dinner.

I don't need to tell you that fluffy promises made en masse are a thing of fantasy.

In reality, the opportunity was a move to the French HQ or the main UK office in Manchester for the non-coding staff if a job existed. Hardly a blue sky. Hardly an opportunity.

One by one, we got called into the boardroom.

One by one, we left with our redundancy letters.

Infogrames acquired DMA Design as part of the take-over.

This meant they would have the rights to all future games, but they could not fully benefit from the jewel in the DMA crown, Grand Theft Auto, as it was already being published by BMG Interactive (latterly Rockstar Games).

As such, Infogrames sold DMA Design to Take-Two Interactive for just $11m in cash, including the assumption of certain bank indebtedness. In 2002, after the release of Grand Theft Auto III, DMA Design was ultimately renamed Rockstar North and became part of the Rockstar Games label.

The Grand Theft Auto franchise continued with Grand Theft Auto IV (2008) and Grand Theft Auto V (2013). Both games are considered some of the best video games ever made, and Grand Theft Auto V became one of the best-selling games ever.

Infogrames closed the Gremlin studio, then known as Infogrames North, in Sheffield less than five years later. Yet, for another ten years or so, Infogrames continued to survive somehow through mergers and acquisitions, at one point taking over and renaming themselves with the infamous gaming brand Atari.

2013 saw Atari SA (formerly Infogrames Entertainment SA) file for bankruptcy protection under French law, while its America Atari subsidiaries filed for Chapter 11.

It was literally *Game Over*.

But for me, things were getting going after a round of interviews. I was packing boxes in my small, rented house in the North when the call came in.

"Harvey, it's Ian at the recruitment agency. They loved you and want to offer you the job. Can you start next week?" he asked eagerly.

If there was ever a tonic to soothe a problem at the right time, this was it.

The journey during my time at Gremlin might have been a rollercoaster but what mattered was the final destination.

I got a great job in product marketing, back where I felt I belonged, in London. I'd missed seeing my parents, sister, and old friends after reconnecting with them. But I'd previously moved to London for a reason, and I had unfinished business.

Little did I realise that the shenanigans were just getting started...

KEY LESSONS IN LIFE AND BUSINESS

LEARN HOW TO PREPARE FOR THE INTERVIEW PROCESS

Interviews are an artificial process in which you must position yourself as the best person for the role. You need to make sure you over-prepare yourself before you go in.

Regardless of your applied experience, citing your achievements, think about the most basic elementary things like being hydrated, having a bottle of water with you *with a lid on* (no spillages!) and, for crying out loud, making sure you don't need the toilet.

I'll share a little secret with you in this less-than-secret forum. The last thing I do before I go for an interview or an important meeting is visit the toilet. It means that I won't need the toilet for another hour. I don't drink much water in the meeting, small sips only. There's nothing worse than having to cross your legs bursting for a wee while you're trying to pitch yourself for a gig.

To read an article I wrote on how to ace an interview and show your brilliance, head to my LinkedIn profile. You can also read many other free marketing articles I've written.

FOCUS ON THE DESTINATION, NOT THE JOURNEY

At this point in the book, you must think that Harvey Lee's life is a soap opera.

I can't deny some colour to my life, but that's only ever been the journey. Often, it's hardest to affect the journey, there are so many external factors that you're not in control of. It's more a matter of how you react to them.

Since my late teens, I've been clear about the desired destination. Every time I got there, I set a new one. And so, the journeys continue.

MANY COMPANIES ARE THEIR OWN WORST ENEMIES

One of the biggest lessons I took from my time at Gremlin was how companies must be more realistic. They had delusions of grandeur in a hot market. But they couldn't meet the expectations. They didn't know what they'd let themselves in for in going public. And they paid a heavy price for it.

As you read on, you'll soon discover that Gremlin Interactive weren't alone in making this mistake...

CHAPTER 18

LIKE A VIRGIN

"**H**i, nice to meet you," I said, shaking hands for what felt like the hundredth time that morning. It was my first day at Virgin Interactive.

"That's Beth, personal assistant for one of the MDs," my new colleague said, glancing over his shoulder. "A word of advice... don't give her your car keys."

"Er, why?" I asked innocently.

"Because if she's off her face on coke, she'll drive it straight through the ground floor window of the office, as she did with the MD's Range Rover," he replied.

Welcome to Virgin Interactive, Harvey! Where rock and roll values are very much alive.

I joined the marketing team, led by someone whose own interview consisted of a glass of champagne in the bar next door. I had a 'proper' interview, but I did get the glass of champagne next door too.

I was relieved that snorting coke in the company bathroom wasn't part of the interview process. It was just something some people did once they had signed their contract. Quite often.

I heard one new starter got so carried away on his first day, which happened to be the company Christmas party, that he got fired. He'd got utterly wasted, danced on tables, smashed glasses, and threw food. Even at Virgin Interactive, that wasn't on for the first day. You had to wait a few weeks, at least!

I joined Virgin Interactive at an essential time for the company. Fresh from a merger [groan] with US company, Interplay, I was one of the 'new breed' to join. Most of the staff previously worked for either Virgin or Interplay, and I was the new meat in the sandwich of alliances.

When you forge a new entity out of two existing entities with distinct attributes, you can expect some conflict. There was a 'them and us' vibe in the company between the two 'former' companies.

I was stuck in the middle. I worked for the 'new' Virgin Interactive, but my portfolio was purely from Interplay, the US products, so I had a balancing act to manage. I was one of four product marketers in the team, so I just set about doing the best for the products without taking sides.

One of my studios was Shiny Entertainment, most notable for titles like Earthworm Jim. And renowned for late delivery of the product. So late that no one ever believed a release date they communicated.

The late delivery of games besieged the video games industry during these days. 'Slippage' was the curse of the industry, and Shiny were the master of it. So, you learnt to work with ambiguous delivery dates, short-shipped assets or, in some cases, next to no assets.

I had a notable PC game in the pipeline called Messiah. The gaming press initially got quite excited about this game when it was first announced. You play a cherub-like character that possesses hosts in the game as you play through the God-like storyline.

However, as the game release date got later and later, the press got more impatient and cynical about the title. We needed to ensure that when it did launch, it launched with impact.

And in typical Virgin Interactive style, we pushed the envelope.

We devised a snappy tagline to ensure that gamers knew you had to possess other characters in the game and control them in ways that would be out of your own character's personality.

The strapline for the campaign was 'What on earth possessed you?'

That in itself wasn't controversial. How we applied it was!

We wanted to show a real-life example of someone being possessed to do something they'd never do to get an impact. So, what did we choose?

An image of the Pope smoking cannabis! With the headline 'What on earth possessed you?'

What on earth possessed the marketing department? I think the context was that representing some pretty cool games like Resident Evil and Dino Crisis that had scary or edgy marketing, we were always looking to push a little bit harder each time.

I remember speaking with the magazine publishing houses at the time. Boy, they shit their pants when they saw the advertising we wanted to place with them. They refused to take it, but after some negotiation, they agreed to publish a 'censored' version of the print ad. We put black rectangles over the Pope's eyes but, in doing so, made him look like a criminal.

By 1998, we were using the internet for essential marketing, so we published the full uncensored version online with a call to action to go online to see it. The ad ran just for one monthly magazine edition before the Advertising Standards Authority (ASA) banned it.

The internal power struggle between the US company Interplay and the rest of Virgin was getting more conflicted. It was clear that each time I visited the Interplay office in the States, they had a growing lack of trust in Virgin.

Such was their wariness, that they wanted their guy on the inside. I *was* their guy on the inside, but I was a Virgin employee. Interplay wanted its dedicated team on its payroll.

As Interplay went about building its own organisation inside an organisation, I was propositioned by Interplay's CMO about crossing over from Virgin's payroll.

I saw an opportunity to grow, build a team, and take more responsibility. I took it.

And after the desk and floor move, I met my new boss.

Matt was a very amiable, larger-than-life American sent over by the top management in California to oversee the European operation as General Manager.

"Hey Harvey, great to meet you. Beer?" Matt said, setting the tone and theme for the next couple of years.

"Sure, you know it's not even lunchtime yet?" I retorted.

I got a knowing wink back as an acknowledgement.

Matt was a top guy, but the key was that he was Interplay's guy and Interplay through and through. He knew how everything ticked and had a direct line to the CEO, Brian Fargo. If Matt phoned Brian, things would happen.

My first job was understanding the landscape, the objectives, and the portfolio. Sales and distribution would still be handled in Europe by Virgin, but now, marketing and general (hands-on) management would be directly controlled by Interplay.

And the marketing was my bit, but this time, more generalist marketing over specialising in product marketing. I was fortunate to spend a ton of time in Southern California, where the office was, and soon came to understand why products from Shiny Entertainment were always late. Their office was virtually on the beaches of Laguna Beach.

I forged strong bonds with my American counterparts, both professionally and socially. Interplay had a family feel to it, and I loved that.

Back in London, my immediate focus was to build the marketing team.

"We need to build a dedicated team for Interplay," Matt stated.

I already knew why, but he laid it out…

"The team at Virgin upstairs are going to do nothing for us but the sales basics, so we need our own marketing team to drive awareness and demand for our products," Matt continued. Despite being a merged company, it felt like a business separation.

My first hire was to bring in a marketing manager. Someone I knew that had great attributes in messaging, and a background in advertising would be a significant asset to have on the team, primarily as I was focused on bringing as much in-house as we could.

In 1999, Virgin spent a ton of money on marketing with other agencies. We simply did not have that kind of money.

The only thing we could not bring in was PR. So, I outsourced it to one of the best-known Gaming PR guys out there. The legendary Doug Johns. Doug knew all the journalists inside out, professionally and socially, so his ability to make things happen got him the job.

The team was built with two game producers (who didn't report to me but sat with us) and a marketing assistant who provided heavy-lifting support.

The fit of the team was initially the most notable thing. Great crack in the office, real biting, sarcastic, sometimes cruel British humour at the fore; work was fun unless you were unfortunate enough to be the victim of the moment.

But my marketing manager was an incredible contributor, especially creatively.

He was in top form when posed with the challenge of addressing a new target audience with what was a very geeky game.

Dungeons & Dragons licenced game Baldur's Gate was a

turn-based role-playing game (RPG) for PC that was a cash cow for Interplay, but the audience was, respectfully, complete nerds.

After many iterations on PC, the company was making a console version of the game on PlayStation. PlayStation is cool, but it's a different audience to the PC one. So, the challenge was how to appeal to a broader gaming audience with a PC nerd fest.

1. Reposition the game as an action-adventure game.
2. Change people's perceptions of RPG and Baldur's Gate.

The first part was internal, and the business case wasn't too hard. Data from research agencies such as GfK in Europe showed that the total addressable market by category on PlayStation was way more significant for Action-Adventure than RPG. By repositioning, we could address more people. It helped that the game was more action-oriented, too, so it wasn't misrepresented.

The second part was more challenging because it was qualitative and, at worst, subjective, depending on whom you spoke to.

The creative approach was to parody well-known consumer-facing slogans in the context of a medieval action-adventure game. The recall we got from these in testing and the level of understanding of what the essence of the game was, was good too. I made the case in the States that in the UK and Europe, we should be talking to this new broader audience in a language they understood. With a narrative outside of Baldurs Gate, we knew what people perceived. And in more general media channels than just the hard-core gaming press.

It was a tough case to fight but one we believed in. And we won the right to run the campaign.

The game was a commercial success, selling over one million units globally across PlayStation 2, Xbox, and GameCube. The high quality of the game won the Academy of Interactive Arts

& Sciences award for "Role-Playing Game of the Year" in 2001, defeating the hot-favourite, Final Fantasy X.

I like to think we contributed to that number.

"Fancy a drink after work, Harvey, to toast our success?" Matt asked.

"I wish I could mate, but I can't tonight. I've got a phone interview with Harry Vanda for my website. He's a legendary co-producer... he did all the early classic albums with AC/DC," I replied, grinning from ear to ear.

"Wow, sounds great. I look forward to listening to it when you post it, see you tomorrow," he said.

My website project took up much of my free time, but I loved every minute. It was an AC/DC website called the AC/DC Resource Centre.

Why did I do this? Well, apart from the fact that I was a nerdy bachelor with an AC/DC habit that constantly needed scratching, AC/DC themselves didn't have an official website. You could say there was a gap in the market!

I had access to people and content that most could only dream of due to my connections in AC/DC's world at the time.

So, when I got a phone call from the Product Marketing Manager at EMI Records, the band's UK label for the 2001 release, *Stiff Upper Lip*, I listened intently.

EMI had been looking for a way to use the power of the internet for the up-and-coming release. However, with the band still being very analogue, in every sense, and not even having their own website, they looked to the fan community.

And they called me. Why me?

At that point, I was getting a quarter of a million unique visitors to the site each month, and I had thousands of email addresses of AC/DC fans from around the world in my database. EMI wanted digital reach, and I had it.

"Harvey, we've got no budget for this digital activity. Digital and the internet here is still very nascent, and no one wants to spend money on it," she offered up in our face-to-face meeting a few days later.

This pitch was hard to swallow when I looked at the EMI offices and the band's sales record! However, I wanted to help, so I made it easy for them.

"I'll give you full access and be your business partner on this, on two conditions," I countered.

She leaned in. "Go on..."

"Number one, you publish my URL on the official advertising for the album."

"Done," she confirmed.

"Number two, I get a gold disc with my name on it. If it doesn't go gold, then a commemorative disc acknowledging my contribution."

She twisted her face. I must've caught her by surprise. She twirled her pencil through her fingers as she audibly hummed to herself whilst staring into space. Clearly looking for some sort of divine sign from above.

"Double done! Let's go to work!" she said a few seconds later. She knew she had no choice if she wanted my help.

We started planning in the EMI offices right then and there.

She got more than she asked for, too. I went to every AC/DC show on the tour and did a tour blog from each show, including some outside the UK borders.

Interplay and Virgin Interactive had offices in Hamburg and Paris, and Matt and I went over for meetings and took in some AC/DC shows simultaneously!

One night, after a show in Hamburg, I went for a drink in the bar of the hotel with our German Product Manager, Taz. It was a hotel we'd stayed in before when on Interplay/Virgin business.

It was *really* quiet.

"Wouldn't it be funny if AC/DC walked in?" I said, joking. And just then, they *did!*

Suddenly, my childhood heroes were at the end of the bar, and I was rooted to the spot. Frozen. I couldn't move. I felt nauseous, and my head was spinning. I knew that in a few seconds, they would be gone. I knew they didn't drink, and I heard a record-company type tell them to wait at the bar whilst they checked on the restaurant.

I had no time. I had to do something. I knew this would be my only chance to get 1:1 time with them. Just them and me.

What should I say? What should I ask? How do I even say 'hello?' Basic human capabilities like walking in a straight line, not puking or speaking words had all vanished from my abilities.

Taz was the voice of reason. "Just say 'hello'… what's the worst that can happen?"

And then, they got up and started walking toward the restaurant door. I was going to blow it. The band had their back to me, and they were getting further away. And then…

I inhaled so deeply that I must have had more air in me than the Stay Puft Marshmallow Man. I jettisoned myself through the air like Keanu Reeves in The Matrix; whilst in motion, I threw the crappy £5 disposable camera in my pocket to Taz and landed, unflustered, in front of Angus Young. Lead guitarist of AC/DC.

"Hello, I'm Harvey. I ran the website for the UK album launch and lent you and George (brother and AC/DC Producer) a copy of *Atlantic* for the *Bonfire* box set. How are you?"

Then a deaf pause, which seemed to last a lifetime to me.

Very fortunately, Malcolm Young, Angus' brother, AC/DC rhythm guitarist and band leader, remembered my help on the *Bonfire* box set and broke out with the first words and a warm greeting.

Man, why did I get myself into such a state? The band were

fantastic, Malcolm and Angus especially. We chatted for a few minutes about things at the UK Alberts office and studio, the tour, and people we knew. The only shame was that singer Brian Johnson had already gone to bed! So much for the Rock and Roll lifestyle!

And crucially, Taz got the photo. And then, like the wind, they were gone.

I think at Interplay, we were more rock and roll than AC/DC, and there was nothing more rock and roll than my birthday weekend in Amsterdam.

Matt never needed an invitation to a party, so when it was suggested that he and my whole team go to Amsterdam for a what-goes-on-tour-stays-on-tour weekend, resistance was nowhere to be seen. We even seemed to pick up a couple of staffers from the US office too.

Anyone who knows anything about Amsterdam is that things can happen legally there that can't happen anywhere else. So, I must stress now that no one broke the law!

'Coffee shops' are one of these things. Well, not for the coffee, you know, but for the 'herbal cigarettes.' It was always going to be a normal state of affairs that beers and smoking too much were part and parcel of the weekend for most.

The women, on the other hand, were a whole different case. Because prostitution is legal. If you've ever been to the Red Light District in Amsterdam, you'll know that it's an Alice in Wonderland of near-naked women in shop windows. And they're actively looking for your business!

To be clear, they didn't find any with me; I chickened out. But I'll never forget the look on the face of a 'customer' coming out after popping his cherry! And he was no spring chicken!

But there was a case to answer for the birthday boy, and the crime scene was The Banana Bar. The first thing I saw was a big sign saying 'no photos.' Believe me, the heavyweight bouncers on the door and inside enforced this policy rigorously.

It was packed inside, and I could see why! In their own words, 'where beautiful girls perform amazing tricks on the long bar.'

And didn't they just! But we were not there to sample fine ales or aged whisky. We were together with a slew of bachelor parties for 'the show.'

The show is a fee-paying experience at the end of the bar, where one of the topless bar ladies would come over and 'perform' for your entertainment. What you didn't know was that *you* were part of the show.

Matt got the cash out and said, "Happy Birthday, Harv. Here's your present!"

My 'host' was a *very naughty-looking* Filipino who promised to "entertain me long time." For the sake of ease, let's call her Destiny because she had my destiny in her hands… actually, it was somewhere else on her body but come on. I'm trying to keep the filth as clean as I can. Destiny didn't take bloody no for an answer either! As she came closer to the chest-height mini stage, my group started pushing me forward to the edge of the stage. They weren't taking bloody no for an answer either!

The show started passively enough, everyone cheering the teasing on, but then…

"Who da Birthday boy then?" she suggestively and provocatively asked.

I didn't say anything, I just got shoved before her. And this is where I learnt where the 'banana' in the banana bar comes from! She made half the banana disappear and, on my hands and knees, I kid you not, I had to make the other half disappear too, but not with my hands, with my mouth!

I'd got an audience, not only of colleagues but about 200

tourists too, and then, due to my apparent apprehension, it started.

"Harvey...Harvey...Harvey," my team started to chant my name!

"Harvey...Harvey...Harvey," the whole bar started to chant my name!

"Harvey...Harvey...Harvey," Destiny started to chant my name!

I was on all fours on the stage, I closed my eyes. **And I made a fruit salad with Destiny,** and once in, the banana turned torpedo and got 'fired' across the bar.

But that's not all; *she* wanted to play. Fucking ping pong. Without table tennis bats.

So, the ball went into the *most talented* part of her body and appeared at 100mph, as it, too, shot across the bar. Then another one bounced off the top of my head, and another one, and another one. She was a one-woman ping-pong machine gun!

At this point, there was a sheer frenzy in the bar, 200 guys jumping, cheering, the girls behind and on the bar all in some sort of sleazy unison. It was disgraceful. It was legal. And it was magical.

"Happy Birthday, big boy," Destiny laughed as she grabbed my...

The morning after the night before saw us return to political changes in the corporate world. A third company, a French company called Titus (oh, here we go again), were sniffing around, and the vibes were that some sort of takeover was in the offing.

We had work to do, so off I went with Doug on a press tour with the founders of leading developer Bioware around Europe, and we got to grips with repackaging and bundling a bunch of our role-playing games.

The latter part was crucial to our operation. The development cycle was long and somewhat unreliable in terms of delivery.

The development team and my team played our role in keeping the revenue and business moving.

For each tier-one landmark game, such as Baldur's Gate 1, we'd have to wait a year or more for a full sequel. But the development team at Black Isle Studios were also good at feeding the RPG community with related games in-between.

Expansion packs and the associated PR kept fans occupied and engaged whilst the next 'big' game was in parallel development. We were feeding the machine.

On our part, we had to market and sell it, even though tier-two games generally sold at a ratio of 1:4 vs tier-one games. So we had very little marketing budget to promote them.

We got creative and bundled the hell out of them. By theme, by value, you name it; we bundled it.

Critically, this gave the sales team upstairs something new to sell and kept our place on the store shelves. That was more important than you might think because, in the late 90s, PC games were sold in packaging the size of a small shoe box! Big downloads were a way off yet.

So, as a sustaining strategy, bundling did its job.

Our distributor in Poland, who also localised the Interplay RPG Games, invited us over to discuss the challenges they had in the business and help us understand a little more about their market.

The business meetings were excellent, especially the market visits. I gained so much from 'getting out of the building', talking to customers, and understanding the nuances of the distribution channel. It changed my outlook on go-to-market planning and all the other steps I needed to work backwards (suitable packaging, localisation, etc.).

And it became apparent that [high] pricing was holding our business back over there. Most of the PC game sales in Poland then were cover mounted on specialist magazines and sold through kiosks on the street. The magazines cost a little more than a regular magazine, but you got a full authentic game included, way cheaper than a fully packaged title in a store.

The alternative would be seeing our [total price] games get counterfeited and sold on the black markets. Which we also visited. We saw our games in these markets that hadn't yet been released!

With the kiosk model, the volume difference was enormous, and our distributor showed us comparable data. Sales of a few hundred or a few thousand could turn to tens of thousands with a change in distribution strategy and lower pricing. And you'd mitigate the counterfeit risk at the same time.

We just had to sell it internally to the US HQ for approval! I could hear the objections in my head before we even left Warsaw, however. "What? You want to sell our best title for $1?!"

The illustrative comparison in value internally was clear, however. If we could 'get over ourselves', we'd make more money and, critically, not be counterfeited.

But first, as a matter of dinner and cultural exchange, we were taken out for a 'Polish experience'... at the American Diner in Warsaw. It didn't feel very Polish until... a large silver tray of Polish vodka shots arrived.

"Na zdrowie" (cheers), and we slammed the shots.

Then another full tray arrives.

"Na zdrowie" (cheers), and we slammed the shots.

"Shall we look at the menu now?"

We ordered, and then another tray of shots came. I think I'd done five shots before the starter. And we did a tray of shots between each of the three courses and a shot for an aperitif.

"Where shall we go now?" Marcin, our noble host, asked.

How about the hospital? I thought to myself. I'm not a drinker.

But it seemed I *could* take it. After what must have been half a bottle of Polish vodka, I didn't feel too bad. I certainly didn't feel out of control... I felt I could play with the big boys... Polish vodka... yeah, no problem.

"We are going to a special club. Come on, let's go!" Marcin announced.

Only, there was a problem. I tried to get up, and my legs were all over the place. Suddenly, my body had forgotten how to stand up and walk. I was like a newborn foal, two minutes old, trying to stand up.

The top half of my body was almost sober; the bottom half was blind drunk.

I was helped into a car, and we went to what I can only describe as an underground club. My last memory of it is that it was some kind of dystopian freak show. I say memory because soon after, I didn't have one.

Introducing the Polish Mad Dog shot (Wściekły Pies); recipe below if you'd like to try this at home:

1. Raspberry syrup
2. Vodka
3. Tabasco sauce

The combination of chilli, strong alcohol, and sweet raspberry is somehow indescribable. The flavour experience might be complex, but the brutal effect isn't. Because after half a dozen of them, my whole body was fully incapacitated.

I woke up at 2pm the following day in my hotel room. Ten hours of my life were missing.

Talk of takeovers got more robust, and I soon learnt that French publisher Titus would own a majority interest in Interplay Entertainment Corp in February. We were all a bit flummoxed by this and wondered what the outcome would be.

I'd only just recovered after the last (French) takeover!

The Electronic Entertainment Expo, or E3, as it's more commonly known, is the annual expo for the global video games industry. We were off to attend, primarily to see what the competition was up to and meet with European partners who also attended.

It was also an excellent opportunity to catch up with colleagues and for me to connect with my (dotted line) boss, the VP of Global Marketing.

As my PR guy Doug and I boarded the Virgin Atlantic flight to LA, I told him I had a treat in my hand luggage.

"Doug, mate, we're not eating the slop they have on the plane; I've brought us our lunch," I bragged.

"Hmm, yeah, what, like a sandwich?" He replied.

"Oh no"... I flashed a shit-eating grin and slowly and carefully started pulling out a brown paper bag with handles on it.

"Hold on! That's a..." and before he finishes –

"Yup!" I proudly stated... "a chicken vindaloo Indian takeaway!"

As I pulled the paper bag out of my rucksack, the smell became very obvious. I have to say, it smelt brilliant but anti-social or what? We were on an 11-hour flight in economy.

As we boarded the flight, I made a beeline for one of the female cabin crew.

"Hi, I have a special diet, and I forgot to tell the airline about my special needs before now. I'm so sorry, but I've brought what I need. Would you be able to heat it up for me?" I asked.

Full of attentive empathy, the cabin stewardess agreed without questions.

"We'll have to do it before the main meals, sir, so once you see the drinks service start, just press the call button, and we'll take care of it for you," she said.

I sat back, gave Doug a wink, and waited for my moment.

At 35,000 feet, my call button goes off, and the stewardess comes over.

After I remind this kind lady of her commitment, I reach

inside my backpack. As the brown paper bag with the Indian takeaway is slowly revealed, I keep my best poker face in place.

As the bag and the truth are revealed, the demeanour of our stewardess changes in real-time from helpful, attentive empathy to sheer abhorrence and acceptance that...

She'd been had. She grabbed the bag and stormed off in a huff.

'She's gonna throw it in the bin, mate," Doug scoffed.

And then, a few minutes later, the smell of warm, comforting, aromatic Indian food started wafting through the plane. Well, less wafting, more like invading.

I saw some passengers rubbing their hands with glee, they thought *they* were in for a treat. The beer glasses got refilled, and the mood lightened.

And we got our full curry served on business class plates. We smugly tucked in... the stewardess turned her attention to the rest of the passengers...

"Pasta or fish, sir?" You've never seen 400 people more disappointed.

Back in the acquisition game, Titus acquired and increased its share in Virgin Interactive Entertainment, meaning they had stakes in both Interplay and Virgin. Who was running the show now?

Well, we didn't have to wait too long to find out because, throughout 2000 and 2001, the group of companies got consolidated. Titus owned the lot but clearly showed that there was no leadership despite ownership.

None of us knew what was going on except what we could see. Budgets were being cut, and key staff were leaving, because the void of communication of any kind of vision or plan was absolute.

In 2001, I got a call from Rose at Microsoft. She'd been allocated Interplay on her account for this new sparkly thing we'd all heard about.

Xbox.

In the first meeting at our offices, she invited me to 'X01', the inaugural pre-launch event in Morocco for Xbox.

But, within a month or so, the world looked very different.

Matt rushed over to our desk area. "Guys! Tiffany just called. A plane just flew into the World Trade Center in New York!"

And as we all rushed next door to Jamie's Bar to watch the live news on TV, the sheer scale of the horror dawned on us. When Tiff called, we thought she was talking about a light aircraft stranded on top of one of the towers.

We wished that was the case. It was only a year before that I had been to the top of the World Trade Center on a New Year's weekend away.

When we arrived at the bar, we saw a hole and all the smoke in the first tower, but we were confused. We couldn't take the magnitude of it in. Until we saw the second plane crash live. Then, the towers came down. We all stood there in silence. Trembling. In complete shock.

Without speaking, we knew the world would never be the same again.

And as reality dawned, its effect on the business world did too. Soon after, I was in LA for work, and with my dark complexion, I started getting stopped by security. Microsoft relocated X01 from Morocco, a place now considered too risky, to Jean-Paul Gaultier's house in France.

I didn't go.

It was all change in the office as well. The corporate rot had well and truly set in with the complete take-over of Interplay and Virgin.

What was left of Interplay pulled back out of having an independent presence in Europe. Matt and his wife moved back to America, and those of us left moved back upstairs to the Virgin offices. There was complete confusion over the future of this new 'Titus Interactive' company. No one, and I mean no one, had any idea what was going on.

I'd had enough of bungled takeovers, but as if it were written in the stars, the recruitment agent who placed me at Virgin called me.

"Harv, I know it's all falling apart over there. I don't know your plans, but I have the brief from Microsoft to recruit for Xbox in Europe. They need one Product Marketer before the Xbox launches in about six months. Do you want me to throw your hat in the ring?" Ian asked.

What do you think I said?

KEY LESSONS IN LIFE AND BUSINESS

LEARN HOW TO BUILD A GOOD TEAM OF PEOPLE, OF LIKE-MINDED PEOPLE

A merger can be like an unhappy marriage of convenience. Everybody loses, and everybody gets caught in the crossfire. At this point, I benefited from it and got the opportunity to build a team and create something impactful. This is where I started to learn how to manage a global organisation for the first time.

MAKE OR CREATE SOMETHING TO MAKE A DIFFERENCE

This was the first time I had an opportunity to build something bigger than just doing work for myself and creating something with multiple people with an impact that I'd be proud of. Yes, we pranked about, drank too much, and had lots of fun, but we created something meaningful that we cared about. I still reflect on some of our work and think it still stands up.

GET A SIDE HUSTLE

The AC/DC Resource Centre was my first real side hustle because the website had been getting noticed, and I got the call from EMI Records off the back of it. They saw the value of how I could help them.

Having a side hustle is good, but make it something you're passionate about and good at. It just so happened in this case; it was about my favourite band. I know plenty of people today with side hustles directly correlated to their day job. My role at the Product Marketing Alliance started as a side hustle with them two years prior to becoming their Vice President.

You could say it was the longest job interview in history!

LIFE IS FULL OF SERENDIPITY

Twelve-year-old me would never have believed that I'd meet AC/DC and perform in the venue I first saw them in, let alone do freelance work for them. Life's journey and the ebb and flow of events you're reading about in this book are all tied together with a serendipitous thread.

Call it luck, if you will, but as you've learnt, whether by design or default, that luck was created from my actions. Serendipity did the rest.

▲ No one knew that it was me who helped the band. Malcolm's note in the lid of the box set reads:

"To Harvey (hope you enjoy)
Thanks for helping out with Live At The Atlantic,
All the best,
Malcolm Young.
AC/DC.
'97"

▲ 1st July 2001, Park Hyatt Hotel. Hamburg, Germany. "Wouldn't it be funny if the band walked in?", I said. Then they did. (L-R front Harvey Lee, Angus Young. L-R back Cliff Williams, Malcom Young [RIP], Phil Rudd).

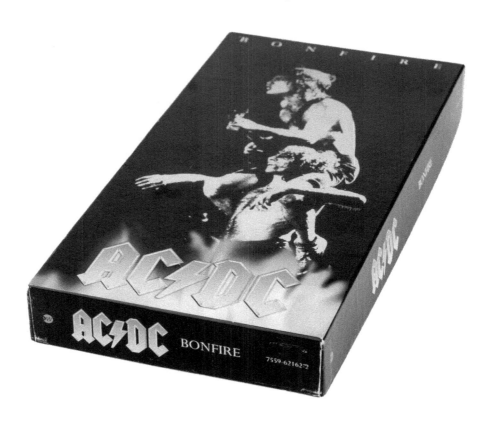

▲ My 'thank you' from EMI Records for helping them with the digital campaign for 2001's *Stiff Upper Lip* album.

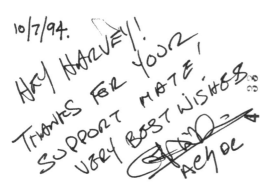

◄ A small unsuspecting envelope drops on the mat. I open it and there's a handwritten thank you note from AC/DC bassist, Cliff Williams.

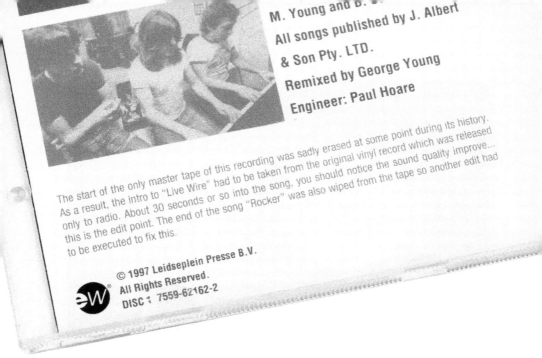

M. Young and B. &
All songs published by J. Albert
& Son Pty. LTD.

Remixed by George Young

Engineer: Paul Hoare

The start of the only master tape of this recording was sadly erased at some point during its history. As a result, the intro to "Live Wire" had to be taken from the original vinyl record which was released only to radio. About 30 seconds or so into the song, you should notice the sound quality improve... this is the edit point. The end of the song "Rocker" was also wiped from the tape so another edit had to be executed to fix this.

© 1997 Leidseplein Presse B.V.
All Rights Reserved.
DISC 1 7559-62162-2

▲ Now you know the full story behind these sleeve notes.

CHAPTER 19

BILLION DOLLAR BABIES

"So, Harvey, the challenge is on! The Xbox is being released in Europe in 90 days, and we can't afford for anything to go wrong. Understand, mate?" Neil said. My boss was affable but as serious as a heart attack.

"Sure," I replied, nodding. I took a big gulp of my coffee and instantly regretted it. It was boiling. I tried to balance the teetering cup as my tongue set on fire.

Earlier the same year, Robbie Bach, Chief Xbox Officer, had been at the E3 convention to give the World Premier of Xbox. He stood up on a very public stage, pressed the Xbox power button and... nothing. It wouldn't work. It wouldn't even turn on.

The world was watching. We were just twelve people, our very own Justice League, and even though there were just over three months between the US and European launch, we still didn't have a single European Xbox in the office.

So, as I sat at my new desk at Microsoft, the scale of our challenges was sharply coming into view. It hit like an oncoming freight train.

The US launch, considering such a backdrop of known and unknown (at the time) challenges, was a spectacular event at

Toys R US in New York City. It was remarkable to think it was only eight weeks since 9/11.

One and a half million Xboxes selling in six weeks put a significant strain on supply, as did DVD drive issues at the factory. But the US launch gave us perceived momentum in Europe, and the case could now be put that Microsoft wasn't out of place in this category.

Another reason it worked was that the launch line-up of games had a significant jewel. Halo: Combat Evolved.

Despite not showing up in the best light at E3 six months earlier, the development team at Bungie Studios had made enormous strides. It delivered a first-person shooter (FPS) game that'd redefine this generation of gaming.

My first week was about orientation to the organisation and the product. The support coming out of HQ at the operational level was very challenging.

"Hi Arthur, great to meet you," I enthusiastically greeted my International Product Marketing Manager, my eyes and ears in the US office.

"Hey, Harvey, I heard you joined, although I don't know why we need your role; why are you here?" his boss Pete retorted.

Hardly a warm, inviting welcome for a first meeting. I soon realised I'd have to do everything myself with very little support, given there was just one junior person stateside to help international markets.

I might've been looking at an inbound freight train; Arthur was the veritable rabbit in the car headlights.

I also learned from flying around our region that many of the staff on Xbox had transferred from other departments within Microsoft. We had people joining the Xbox team from diverse unrelated backgrounds who knew very little about video games.

This was a start-up in many respects. Every day was a huge challenge. Things were cobbled together to get the job done.

Even down to basic things like being able to send a large file had become an operational root canal, and I slept under my desk more than once whilst waiting on critical files to transfer slowly to and from the US.

Is this how you perceived it? No, me neither.

The pain points quickly focused on processes, tools, and assets. There were practically none. Pragmatism over perfection was called for. But, one by one, we got it together, and at the last minute, we got some European products.

The European launch was coming into view fast, the broadcast of a European-only TV advert, nicknamed 'Champagne', being the starting pistol that got us underway.

"Life is Short, Play More," the tagline professed as it depicted a baby being born, shooting out of the mother in labour, flying through the air; the baby soon aged in front of your eyes into an old man and landed in a grave! Life really was short – about 30 seconds, by this example.

But it was a great ad and more than served its purpose of announcing that Xbox had arrived. Before it went on to win a host of awards and then get banned.

The Xbox campaign in Europe was based around the proposition that we should play more in life because of various living conditions, such as life is short, life sucks, etc. The follow-up TV ad, nicknamed 'Mosquito', even finished with the statement, 'Life Sucks, Play More.'

The expectation built on the initial success in the US was high, and the team set about a great launch day in the UK. March 14th, 2002, will forever be ingrained in my memory.

"Hey, it's starting!" shouted Harry, our advertising manager.

We congregated around a massive screen in the London office, beers in hand, to watch the premiere of 'Champagne' during a high-profile Champions League football game.

This was the moment. And then, 30 seconds later, it was over.

"Harry, that was incredible; the ad really stood out in the football segment!"... we all congratulated him. He'd done a great job and deserved to feel proud.

Then, after all the backslapping, we headed down to the Virgin Megastore in the centre of London for the launch event.

It was like a postcard from the future for every Apple iPhone launch that was yet to come. Queues of people down the street were waiting to get in, and bouncers were pumping music everywhere. You'd swear Michael Jackson had just popped in for a cup of tea and a chat.

Our merchandisers had dressed the huge three-floor store up in Xbox green and put demo machines wherever they could. This was a glittering pop-culture moment. And the moment became of national significance when Sir Richard Branson, the ever-mercurial ringmaster, showed up to hand over the first Xbox sold in the UK in his Virgin store. We were all over the newspapers the following day.

The team made it happen despite all the concerns and challenges. But it wasn't long before the concerns turned to real market problems.

The Xbox launched with a hefty price tag of £299 in the UK and $299 in the US. Despite the rush out of the gate, the good initial sales we got were, in fact, just pent-up demand from months and months of pre-launch marketing.

The expected launch momentum didn't materialise. In the US, the downward curve took a little longer, but in Europe, we dropped off the end of a cliff in just the second week. So profound was the drop that we had panicked retailers on the phone asking, "what are you going to do now?"

We didn't know. We'd expected better momentum and failed to plan for any other outcome. There was no plan for this scenario beyond the launch.

The US had had just five months of sales when they dropped

the price from $299 to $199. That's an almighty price drop so soon after launch and an admission that the launch price was too steep for our position in the market. It was also the moment that the whole project got put further into the red because with this new price, every Xbox sold would now lose about $225, given the high cost of manufacture and the revised lower sales forecasts.

That alone would end up being an unforeseen $5.5 BILLION loss. For most companies, this would have been an immediate Chapter 11 filing.

This put Europe in an even trickier position, we had only just launched a month earlier, and the US, the only market bigger than ours, had dropped their pants on the price. Even though our price match with the US would eventually come, we had to find a way to bridge the gap and stimulate sales.

Our GM, Tom, got the approval to bundle two free games in Europe with the console, and this did buy us time. And some sales.

But nothing is that simple is it? You can't just give away over £75 worth of games soon after the console launch and expect all the early adopters to be OK with it, can you? To ensure that parity was restored and that we looked after this hugely important cohort, we ran a program to supply those same games to them for free.

Yours truly had to devise a program and manage the distribution of thousands of free games without the power of the internet as we know it now. It was done with the power of Excel, Post-It notes, the Royal Mail postage service and a ton of manual labour and internal alignment.

The biggest issue holding up sales was the roadmap of compelling games themselves. The launch lineup was good, three titles especially, but when you consider that a hardcore gamer plays a new game every six weeks, this becomes a problem.

For a year after launch, nothing genuinely compelling or original showcased the Xbox's power, the main unique selling point for the console. We were launching cross-platform games that were also released on Sony's PlayStation 2 and Nintendo's GameCube, with only slight variations from the other versions. It wasn't enough to get gamers to leave what they knew and play Xbox.

In the meantime, we had to work with what we already had, but even that had its challenges.

Halo was *so* central to our portfolio that it was almost at the expense of everything else, especially on first-party games. However, shooting games in many parts of Europe are nowhere near as popular as they are in the US. The further south in Europe you go, the less popular they become.

Football and racing were the most popular genres in countries like Italy and Spain.

We didn't have a football title on Xbox. We had one genuine racing game. Europe couldn't rely on Halo alone if we were going to break Southern European markets. The sales curve reflected it, the retailers were telling us as much.

Spain was a strategically important market. It was PlayStation's stronghold in Europe, doing disproportionally high numbers. FIFA Football was the top-selling game, and the console's price was attractive for its positioning.

Sony was very clever at this part. They played the regional differences well, but they also played to their format as a more general consumer electronics and media-owning juggernaut. For example, in Spain, Sony cross-marketed the PS2 as an affordable DVD player, with household DVD penetration having headroom. It was more cost-effective to buy a PS2 than many DVD players themselves! Sony had a channel presence in the Movie and TV aisle due to its ownership of Columbia Pictures and its TV manufacturing business.

With the PlayStation 2, Sony played across not just games but movies and TV and was very influential in markets like Spain at bringing it all together and pooling their marketing resources.

The team in our Spanish office felt the pain.

"Hola Harvey, let's take you on store visits in Madrid, show and explain to you the unique challenges we have," Manuel, our marketing lead, would propose.

So, we'd spend half a day driving around El Corte Ingles, Media Markt, and Carrefour, to name but three.

"You see, Harvey, we're well represented next to Sony and Nintendo, but we're not competitive on pricing, bundles, and available games. We're pulling every favour Microsoft can muster, but we can't compete budget-wise," Manuel explained.

He was right. We didn't have the diversity of offers or presence in the TV aisle that Sony did, and we certainly didn't have the people, deep local distribution or budget of Sony.

We were getting put to the sword, and Halo wasn't the answer.

Knowing all this, the case was made back in the office that we had to start to segment and prioritise our content to the right markets. Not just go with the Global plan. Moreover, we had to make it easier to market and more cost-effective for our audience.

And so, an idea was born. Hard bundle *relevant* content for all or different markets or even specific retailers so we could lead with an appropriate content-first strategy rather than trying to market the games and console separately. After all, the console itself is just a conduit to deliver great gaming experiences.

So, I put them together.

The economics weren't too tricky for first-party games. After number crunching, we concluded that if we charged just 50% of the price of the total game price, not only would we be more competitive, but if we got the volume break, then even with estimated cannibalisation, we'd make *more* money than selling the console and game separately.

An attach ratio of a particular game to a specific number of consoles sold would move from 5-10% to 100%. We just had to prove our assumptions worked for real.

The biggest internal challenge was how we packaged it. I insisted that we first needed an entirely new packaging design leading with the game identity. The Xbox brand team insisted that the Xbox brand mandatories and console image were the most important thing and could not be changed.

Something *had* to change because the whole of the packaging was brand mandatories and console image.

We had chosen Project Gotham Racing 2 as the game to focus on in Spain. This was a logical choice based on the popularity of the genre there and the high quality of the game. The concept was to turn the creative of the console box into the bonnet of a Ferrari, which was the feature car from the game.

But the brand police had a hissy fit, specifically Miss Self-Appointed Steward of all brand police matters in Europe, Wilhelmina Woodward.

"How dare you! You, *you* trash the Xbox console brand!" she'd shout louder and louder as she chased me around the desks in the office, trying to get me to take her seriously.

It was hard to take her seriously.

"Have you seen the latest research? Brand tracker? What you're proposing is just reckless!" she'd shout.

"I've seen it, Aunt Willie. If you drill down to the country level, you'll see what I see and that it supports my business case," I replied. She hated being called Aunt Willie.

And as her eyes went all googly and foam came out of her mouth, she'd follow me into the elevator, pointing her finger at me like a pistol.

"Your career's over, if you try to get this approved!"

It got approved.

Looking at the numbers, doing nothing wasn't an option.

After multiple calls with brand folks, it came down to two fundamentals. The Xbox logo on the pack and the presence and position of the Xbox Nexus (to you and me, that's a circle with an X in it!). If I preserved these, then they'd give me some latitude.

Ferrari wouldn't allow us to include their logo on the red bonnet, so we got creative. We made a generic red bonnet in a Pantone shade half a click away from Ferrari's brand colour and kept the green Xbox Nexus in the middle of the bonnet. And wrote everything in Spanish, not English. We positioned it internally as something to learn from, and it got approved in Seattle because this was a pilot. Much to Aunt Willie's visible displeasure.

Ladies and Gentlemen, start your engines! El Pack Roja Furia (The Red Fury Pack) was born!

The manufacturing run of 5,000 units sold easily enough but critically sold through to consumers well. It not only got over the finish line but also sold out on all stock and did a victory lap around key Spanish retailer El Corte Ingles.

We developed a new impactful marketing programme out of what we had. The boxes marketed themselves at a local tactical level; the bundle program expanded beyond anyone's expectation to third-party publishers and enriched game marketing to the point where they increased game revenue beyond what a game could sell by itself. So much so, that by 2012 (ten years later), 50% of console sales in EMEA were attributed to hard (repackaged) bundles, and that Xbox was still following the same strategy at the time of writing.

We'd contested a battle, but the console war was just getting going.

KEY LESSONS IN
LIFE AND BUSINESS

WE WERE PREPARED FOR LAUNCH, BUT WE WEREN'T PREPARED FOR ANYTHING ELSE

We put all our eggs in one basket. We assumed that having an enormous launch would give us enough momentum to get us into orbit. We were wrong.

The first week, the plan was to just push more, but it became evident very quickly that wasn't going to work. The market just handed our asses to us on a plate. It saw through the holes in our plan and was unforgiving.

We were genuinely trying to learn this business from scratch in real time. But we thought we knew enough. Right? Maybe we knew enough but didn't have the right portfolio, timing, pricing, etc. It doesn't matter how big the company is, it can still get its ass handed to it on a plate because the market is *the* force to be reckoned with.

THE BIGGER THE REPUTATION, THE HARDER THEY FALL

Aunt Willie was recognised as a rising star in the company. She had a big reputation but couldn't have been a squarer peg trying to fit into a round hole.

'Willie' was used to getting her way all the time. But she was part of a growing European team, and you must work well with people.

She struggled in this regard, and not getting her way quickly led to ways of working that felt like she was working against us and not with us. She eventually got burned by her own projects when, allegedly, it turned out she misrepresented research data to get her way.

CHAPTER 20

HEART-SHAPED (X)BOX

"**L**ads, get your passports; we're heading to Seville for X02!" I announced at the team meeting, unwittingly stating what most people already knew.

"Harvey, Harvey, Harvey..." they replied, taking the piss. I'd never live down my time at the Banana Bar, would I?

We needed another event to show the games industry the path forward for Xbox since we launched it. We had to inject enthusiasm into the platform by showing people what we had coming.

"So, we're going to invite retailers, press, and critically, third-party publishers to join us in Seville, Spain, for a big day at a theme park. Hired, closed, and branded in green just for us."

X02 was to be epic. As well as the free rides for attendees to enjoy, there'd be future games on display, big plans, and news shared at keynotes by leadership and workshops for developers. It was all set to show the path forward and encourage further support for Xbox.

All the big guns were out in force, and it was a demonstration by Microsoft that Xbox meant business. Despite the challenges, it was a determined display that Xbox was making progress and was here to stay.

This was in full evidence when two brand new Volvo articulated lorries turned up, custom painted in Xbox colours and trailers converted to mobile Xbox demo stations. The marketing guys bought these two trucks to drive around Europe and provide demos on demand. No expense spared.

The event itself was a great success but the thing that I recall the best, even to this day, was the after-show party for Xbox staff. It was the main course of hedonistic banging music, and alcohol, with a palpable release of tension on the side. There was a vibe of anything goes. And literally, anything did.

The top management all dressed as Che Guevara, normally reserved staff loosened up to the point of (and some beyond) HR violation, and senior regional and US leaders got *so* drunk that dribbling on yourself whilst half-cut became mandatory. We were force-feeding each other champagne straight out of the bottle, girls I work with started kissing each other, and more and more naked flesh was being put on display.

It was a full-on rave that became legendary within Xbox circles. Even at the time, blitzed out of our minds, we all knew it would become an 'I was there' moment.

But despite the flow of energy, at breakfast the next morning, the vibe changed dramatically. Rumours were abounding that our GM was in trouble with HQ – not because of the party per se but because of the performance and perceived the way Xbox was being run as an unaccountable autonomous island in Europe.

Soon after X02, he was gone. The spiritual and cultural leader we'd known and followed was no more.

Seattle was replacing him with a 'trusted' corporate 'numbers' man. He introduced a fresh rigour to the business, but he sucked the life out of the team completely. His first action was building an office for himself *within* the open plan office, an office he hardly ever came out of. He rarely spoke to anyone who didn't directly report to him, and he never addressed the team.

We were clearly not worthy.

We just got on with the job amidst what would turn out to be many re-organisations. We saw people leave, including Aunt Willie, who'd been on one ill-advised crusade too many. I got re-orged into a new focus region in EMEA, called CSE – Central and Southern Europe.

I'll give Mr. Corporate credit for one thing; he brought more accountability and rigour to the numbers.

My first contact with this was on a flight to Athens with my closest colleague Harry for a business review weekend. Our boss, the Director for the newly formed CSE region, was also under pressure to show a more robust skill set in numerical terms.

"Here's you go, boys, take a look at these," he said to us at 35,000 ft.

"Read through, familiarise yourself, and let me know if you have any questions," a wry smile followed.

"Hey," I whispered to my workmate. "Do you understand this, it looks like the fucking Matrix?"

Harry just gave me a fearful stare back.

This was our welcome to the corporate scorecard. A concept in business and number management I'd come to rely on and be judged on for the rest of my career in multinationals.

In this very specific case, there was a very silver lining. The business review was on a two-day sailing offsite around the Greek Islands. Never mind Life's Short, Play More; this was Play First, Work Later. Much later.

Our boss had spent £10,000 on hiring two 40ft sailing yachts for 'team building.' The only 'work' that we had to undertake was the reviews, and they took place at the bow of the boat.

Each country manager was called to the bow on the hour every hour to explain their quarterly performance. There was nowhere to hide, literally. Your only option was to talk or walk the metaphorical plank.

Despite the incredible scenery, the tone and expectations were set. Rigour around the numbers was now forging as business as usual.

The other thing that was forged was the relationships around our countries. We had Spain, Italy, Netherlands, Belgium, Portugal, Greece, Austria, Switzerland, etc. Thus, brilliant locations for team meetings.

The countries all got on well, and being in a collective with focus helped, but I was shocked to witness a mild-mannered country manager push another country manager into the harbour on the Greek island of Hydra.

I heard him sprinting along the jetty, screaming, "Das hast du dir verdient, du bastard!" (You deserve this, you bastard!) like a wailing banshee, and then...

Fuelled by too much Ouzo and an underlying resentment, he took his chance for revenge. I vividly recall seeing him pass the porthole of my bunk on the yacht headfirst and... splash! It wasn't just that he was purposefully pushed into the water that was funny, it was that our mild-mannered country manager thought it was extremely funny that he was visibly hurt.

Much was forcefully said in German between them. I guess that was the end of a friendship that never really began.

2004 saw the release of highly rated Xbox exclusives Fable and Ninja Gaiden. Both of these games would become big hits. Halo 2 followed later that year and became the highest-grossing release in entertainment history globally, making over $125 million on its first day and becoming the best-selling Xbox game worldwide.

Halo 2 had a day-and-date hard bundle the day the game was released, a practice that took root and is still in operation at Xbox to this day.

And as we got into our rhythm, the consoles then started to come in our rhythm, the consoles then started to come in special colours. First translucent green and then a European exclusive, the see-through 'Crystal Console' which sold 20,000 units very quickly and went to a second production run of another 20,000 units.

But, despite doing everything we could, sales overall were constantly disappointing. Six million unit sales of consoles in Europe from a standing start might sound like a lot, but the high cost of manufacturing the console and lower-than-expected price point put pressure on the financial viability of Xbox.

North America did better with 16 million console sales, but there was a crucial component to this.

The games roadmap had improved, but we *still* didn't have the best-selling third-party games on Xbox in Europe, such as FIFA Football. Halo had done wonderful things, but its outstanding success had brought limitations in Europe especially.

As such, Xbox was perceived as the 'Shooter box', a console primarily for shooter games. And who could argue? If you weren't into Halo or shooter games, what did Xbox have for you? This was born out of the fact that in this console lifecycle, 50% of people who bought an Xbox bought Halo.

The unintentional positioning of Xbox as a Shooter box was now forged in data and undeniable.

Sooner than anticipated, in 2005, it was announced that Xbox would be phased out and replaced with a new model. As far as Microsoft was concerned, nursing a loss of somewhere between $5-$7 billion, this particular war was truly lost.

The question for us was, what was next? What would be different?

KEY LESSONS IN
LIFE AND BUSINESS

YOU NEED TO SELL YOURSELF
TO THE TRADE FIRST

X02 was a coming-of-age event for Xbox in the eyes of the industry. That was the moment that the industry started taking us seriously. And, of course, that was our objective.

It was hosted in Spain because we were failing in Spain, the right games, all the big hitters from the US office flew over, and all the publishers we had supported us.

We painted a vision and were able to demonstrably show it. It was a big success from an industry point of view because it answered so many of the questions people had about us.

From then on, from an industry point of view, we gained much credibility and became a genuine contender in their eyes. We'd launched the product, but X02 was really the starting point.

WE LIVE IN A RESULTS-DRIVEN WORLD

The mood music changed after Tom left. He was the spiritual leader of the team as well as the actual leader of the team. He was hard-drinking, hard-working, and hard-talking, but we didn't have the results.

This taught me that no matter how much you're liked by your team, how much work you put in, how great people think you are, and how much the market loves you, it doesn't matter. We all live in a results-driven world. Nothing else matters.

You can trade on your other attributes for a limited period of time, but all it does is buy you time. Then at some point, the music stops. And this is when Tom's music stopped. And we were all terribly sad to see him go.

WORK FOR YOUR MANAGER,
NOT THE LOGO ABOVE THE DOOR

We market and sell products and services but ultimately, we work with people. And ultimately, from a practical perspective, we work for our manager, not the logo above the front door.

I've been at various companies and loved my manager, but when they moved on (or were moved on), and I inherited a different manager, there were times I thought I was at a different company. Sometimes it was better. Sometimes, way worse.

The relationship with your direct manager is the most important you'll have. Nurture it, grow it, and learn from it.

CHAPTER 21

I CAN SEE CLEARLY NOW

"**W**e're going to announce the new Xbox and soft-land the current Xbox in the market at the same time," Robbie Bach announced to the company in a town hall meeting.

The market had other ideas. Knowing a new version was coming, there was a crash landing fast approaching the horizon. It was time for yours truly and our sales and marketing teams to scramble!

Markets move on very quickly when obsolesce is looming. Despite our best efforts to ensure people knew the original Xbox was still a good investment and would be supported for years. Heck, I'm not sure even we believed that!

You can understand why Microsoft wanted to move on quickly.

How would you feel if you lost nearly $7 billion, three times more than you expected to lose? How would you frame less than 2% market share in one of the top markets, in this case, Japan, to shareholders? If you got outsold 4:1 in Europe, how would you react? Would you even still be in business? Would you have the appetite to go again? Could you even get out of bed?

The fact that Microsoft did was a miracle. Only Microsoft could likely afford to go again.

But what would be different?

We lived for Project Xenon, the code name given to the new Xbox, and after much soul-searching and learning, the proposition and the planning began in earnest.

'Xenon,' with its connected experiences and HD-ready capability, would be well positioned to leverage these key trends, and the organisation set a path to win.

Europe, where I sat, was a second-class citizen in the organisation; consequently, the focus, resources, and results were second-class too. Amongst other initiatives, Project Atlas, the global marketing plan, sought to address this.

By having a unified global plan with regional and well-resourced execution focused on winning in Europe, we moved from a scattered group to a unified team all revolving around a common goal.

"We have the console this time, we have the right games for Europe, we have the price point, and what's more, we have the right path to win," bellowed one of the Global team to a briefing room full of European Xboxers.

"We're going to win this thing [next console war] in the next two years!" he proudly proclaimed as he introduced my manager, Mike.

"Pssst, Harv, have you seen Mike today?" Harry whispered to me.

"Come to think of it, I haven't," I replied.

I rang him. I texted him, but no reply.

I had to sneak up to the stage and ask the presenter to skip to the next speaker without telling him we'd lost Mike.

Then I got a text message. It read...

"Harv, banging hangover, lost my glasses, I can't see jack shit, come downstairs. Mike."

I was greeted with a shell of the person I once knew as my manager. And he couldn't see a thing.

"Let's get you upstairs. I know a door to the room where we can sneak in. Then I'll escort you to the stage. Can you still do your talk?" I asked.

"Yes," he said unconvincingly.

He just about pulled it off and made a good point of reiterating that we had to win the next two holiday seasons.

The Two First Holiday Campaigns (FTHC) became the rallying call we all had to answer. The logic was sound and grounded in market data. The critical insight to winning FTHC was that no console had won a generation two generations in a row when there were three competitors in the market. **As a consequence, the first to 10 million consoles sold would win the whole generation.**

The internal briefing for 'Atlas' was a significant move because global and regional teams came together in a previously unseen way. Senior appointments, including industry veteran Peter Moore, were being made to bolster the cavalry.

Peter's consumer marketing savvy made a huge difference; this was obvious for all to see.

The Xbox 360 was publicly revealed during an MTV special, as opposed to the standard reveal to the trade at the annual E3 Expo in LA.

Everything about what was now known to be the Xbox 360 was different. Marketing, sales, the proposition around connected online experiences, and high definition looked like *leading* the competition, not trying to *catch* it.

The XO events were now Xbox annual industry get-togethers where significant announcements to the trade would be made. If X02 in Seville, Spain, was about ensuring that Xbox was here to stay, X05 in Amsterdam took on a much deeper meaning.

X05 was a regional event turned into a global event to ensure the whole industry knew how important Europe was to Xbox. We flew in hundreds of guests from around the world.

"You're here to work and not to enjoy the unique and enticing benefits Amsterdam offers," Chris, our new GM, briefed us.

"We're all representatives of Microsoft Corporation, and we have to behave as such," he continued.

But this was Xbox, and the somewhat irreverent era of the original Xbox was still very fresh to many of us. A core of us had a creative background pre-Xbox, so going places like Amsterdam was a birthright more than a business trip.

The direct threats from the management of consequences should we dabble in Amsterdam's delights were clear and were adhered to by some. Many choose a different path. I chose a different path, and the night before the primary day, small groups of Xbox staff ninjas spread out across the city, agreeing not to congregate into noticeable groups.

Blending into the night of the town wasn't so tough, and we factored that if we bumped into a member of the senior leadership team in a coffee shop (you know they don't just sell coffee in there, don't you?), then we'd be even, and there's a mutual risk that cancels itself out.

Getting back into the hotel was trickier.

We were staying at The Hilton, where John Lennon and Yoko Ono famously staged their 'Bed-ins for Peace' in 1969. The atrium and bars were crawling with Xbox staff and guests.

"Pete," I whispered.

"Yesh..." he slurped.

"My face is melting, my body is made of jelly," I stated, as I looked around the hotel lobby at hundreds of guests and staff.

"Maybe no one else will notice..." I thought to myself.

Time for ninja action. We broke into groups of two, one to look out and one to make a beeline to the lift. As we quietly giggled our way into an empty lift, we turned with our backs to the walls, breathing out heavily. We'd done it!

No, we hadn't.

As if in slow motion, a giant hand came around the side of the closing doors to stop them from closing. *Shit!*

It was Mitch Koch, Global VP of Sales and Marketing.

A visceral instinct not to get reprimanded (or worse) kicked in, I felt my jelly legs turn to stone and my giggles sober up in an instant. I managed to get a deadpan 'Evening Mitch' out as he turned around with his back to us.

I could never work out if he gave us a pass or if he was as bladdered as the invited journalists were. We never heard of it again, which was a good job because there were previous rock and roll misdemeanours that are still 'secrets of Xbox' that I can't write about. Even twenty years later.

X05 was where we proved our case. All the key announcements, the humility to admit mistakes publicly, the top games available to play, the key pillars of connected experiences, and a future in high definition were all brought to life.

Xbox 360 was a well-designed and thought-out console; hitting the needed price points inevitably had to factor in compromises. Amongst others, two key hardware compromises were that there was no Wi-Fi built in, and the optical drive was a DVD drive, *not* a Blu-Ray Drive (HD).

It was decided internally that HD games could be delivered on the standard DVD9 format with the right compression technology, which helped keep the box's retail cost down. At X05, Chief Xbox Officer Robbie Bach had to answer questions about Microsoft's support for Toshiba's HD-DVD format over Sony's Blu-Ray new proprietary HD media format. A format war between tech giants was getting underway.

And as 'the hardware guy' in Europe, I was in the middle of it.

Xbox had decided not to include the HD-DVD drive in the console. We weren't the rights holder; it'd increase costs, and should the HD format of choice become Blu-Ray, then every Xbox 360 sold to that point would become an albatross. Xbox made an HD-DVD accessory for the console to keep all options open. But not committing it massively diluted the ammunition that Toshiba would need to take on Sony.

On the other hand, Sony committed *all* of its resources to make Blu-Ray successful. They consciously decided to include a Blu-Ray drive in every PlayStation 3, making the PS3 the best value Blu-Ray player you could get at the time. That was a massive commitment and a massive point of value.

But as always, content is king. Without significant support from the movie studios, any format would struggle. You'd expect Sony's movie studios wouldn't support their rival HD-DVD format. Still, after shifting alliances from retailers and studios like Warner Bros, who later decided to drop support for HD-DVD in 2008, Toshiba was left in a very anaemic position at best.

By the time the install base of PS3s hit 10 million, Toshiba had pulled the plug on HD-DVD.

Back in the launch window, the decision to include a Blu-Ray drive in every PS3 took its toll on Sony. We at Xbox had expected Sony to suck up the higher cost, but when it was announced that PS3 would retail at $200 *more* than the Xbox 360 and ship *a year later,* we knew that winning in that first holiday was a real opportunity given Sony's new PS3 wouldn't be in the market.

So much went right for the Xbox 360 during its 2005-2012 lifecycle. It was a time when the product didn't just scale in the market but where organisational and personal growth came to the fore. Many who joined in the early days had either fallen by the wayside, been pushed overboard or, as I and many others did, had scaled with and to the challenges.

"There goes body bag 67," I'd morbidly joke to Harry as another person involuntarily left the company. I lost count after 100.

Not every senior appointment was as successful as Peter Moore's. In 2006, a former executive of Daimler-Benz joined with great internal fanfare, a fanfare that quickly turned to ridicule.

At our annual kick-off event at the Seattle Sheraton, he misjudged the room *badly* in his highly anticipated keynote in front of 1,000 Xbox staff.

"I want to get you motivated," he declared. "Let's split the room in half, up on your feet! Left side, let's shout out, *'Get more sales!'* Right side, when the left side is done, you shout, *'Let's get them now!'"*

And as he proceeded to work the room by enthusiastically waving to each side for their cue, he saw 1,000 Xbox staff reluctantly going along with it. He *must* have quietly felt the error of his ways.

Cheap sales rally tricks are beneath the position of a Microsoft Corporate Vice President. Someone spoke to him during the day about this, and when he closed the event later that day, he was full of remorse onstage as he apologised to 1,000 people.

His reputation never recovered. Two years later, he was in the Xbox body bag.

This was the most significant period of professional growth I'd been through, and the organisation's capability scaled in depth and breadth. Personal development was also now being supported and encouraged by the Xbox management.

Recognising the high quality of consistent content coming through and the need to keep the marketing engine moving all the time, the bundle plan scaled from being an excellent tactic to hold the original Xbox roadmap together to a well-defined plan to grow footprint, support the pillars and drive the hardware engine of the business.

The console business has a very seasonal dynamic, with 60%

of the hardware business done in the last four months of the calendar year.

The operational impact was huge. Delivering over 50% of the console volume as repackaged bundles meant over one million units having to be planned for content, forecasted, and contracts signed with publishers. Moreover, my most crucial internal relationship in this regard was with the Microsoft Ireland Operations Department (MSIOL).

They were the team tasked with physically making it happen. In 2005/2006, they had to rework 450,000 Xbox 360 consoles to include a slew of different games in different languages, adding over 60-100 other items to the price list (SKUs). There were 27 dedicated production lines with 300 staff and an annual operating budget of €4,000,000.

The cost was significant, but the value back to the business far outpunched it. By the time my 12 years at Xbox were up, the annual revenue on the P&L for my business line on all hardware was $1.5 billion.

The systematic operation that became (and still is) the bundle plan earned me my Xbox nickname.

"Harvey, I anoint thee, The Bundle King." Rob in third-party publishing would decree... after my 'coronation,' the nickname stuck.

The business was growing, our professional growth was keeping pace, and then – out of the blue – my personal life changed beyond all recognition.

"What's your story?" asked the pretty, petite brunette at lunch.

And with these three simple words, my world changed. Soon I'd have a serious girlfriend and, within a year, a wife. Natalie was the soul mate I never expected to meet. We were two peas in a pod; we shared a love for music, laughter, and family.

We travelled, shopped and discovered a world together, and for the first time in my life, at the age of 39, I had a life outside of work.

Back at work, the active part of planning was in full swing, and it played well to one of my core capabilities: being very well organised. The bundle program afforded me some memorable moments; the highlight might have been an Abbey Road recording studios event to launch The Beatles Rock Band game in 2009.

"You guys are the new rock and roll, aren't you?" said the guy next to me in the presentation.

"Hi, I'm Giles, Giles Martin."

He got up and started addressing the studio full of eminent industry folks.

Giles worked on The Beatles Rock Band game, and he took us through how it was made, how the old tapes were compiled, and how the gaming experience was put together. It was impressive stuff. But then, no one was more qualified, Giles was Beatles producer George Martin's son!

Taking it all in, we were sitting in the actual studio where the band recorded all their hits; I was sitting next to George Harrison's (RIP) wife. I just needed Paul McCartney to walk in and buy me a coffee, and my day would have been complete!

In this console generation, Nintendo was the surprise package. No one, not even the highest level in our global SLT, saw them coming. Sony didn't see them coming as the Nintendo Wii took the world by storm.

Compared to PS3 and Xbox 360, the Wii was low-fidelity and priced accordingly. This mattered little as they nailed a user proposition and experience with hand-held motion controllers that lit up people's imaginations and tapped into the more casual segments that neither Sony nor Microsoft could go at.

Retrospectively to the Wii launch, the Xbox 360 Kinect was our motion controller. You held nothing; *you* were the controller. The camera technology lit up the concept of the proposition, and dedicated games for Kinect added a new dimension to our effort.

The Kinect, with its reported $500,000,0000 (yes, half a billion!) marketing budget, set the Xbox 360 as a platform alight, reflected in it becoming the fastest-selling gaming peripheral of all time, according to the Guinness Book of Records.

And despite the apparent boost in selling consoles to new segments, Kinect had significant challenges around its core proposition.

Kinect required dedicated games, and the reality was that the roadmap for content was sorely lacking. Of the titles that did support Kinect, there was no depth to the experience, and many games ended up just not being as fun as they should have been. One version of a great Sesame Street game came out, but poor sales led to subsequent versions being cancelled, and so it went.

Most of the games were targeted at the mass casual market, and as such, the Kinect was shunned by the core gamer audience. There was simply nothing in Kinect for them.

Technical challenges also presented themselves. The ambient lighting required for the device to see you effectively went against how most people light their houses, but the other issue was somewhat cultural.

In the US, living rooms and spaces tend to be bigger than in other countries. In Europe and especially Japan, living areas are at a premium, and Kinect needs a certain amount of square footage for you to move around. Reports of customers bumping into furniture or, worse still, putting their foot through a TV screen resulted in us placing a measurement disclaimer on the packaging.

As the Platform Product Marketing Manager for Xbox, even I didn't have enough room at home to use it. Oh, the irony.

And so, it came to pass. Poor content, challenging play spaces, and a Nintendo Wii that 'just worked' meant the world's fastest-selling gaming peripheral became *our most troublesome product* internally. We got to a point where we couldn't sell it after a while unless we trashed the price. Retailers wouldn't take it anymore unless it were on fire sale.

Kinect might have been the most troublesome product, but unfortunately, it wasn't the most problematic issue.

"Harvey, we're getting customer calls from all over Europe on an alarmingly frequent basis, way above normal. They're all reporting the same issue," Chris in customer care gave it to me straight.

"We've escalated on our side, but anything you can do on your side helps. This issue is not going away," he proclaimed.

Reports were coming in thick and fast from consoles showing the three red lights of the four available activity lights on the front of the console. The lighting construct was that each wireless controller connected (with a maximum of four simultaneously connected) would each light up a green quadrant. These lighting quadrants also lit up in red should there be an error, with different combos of red quadrants lighting up to tell you about a specific error.

Many errors could be fixed there and then. Simple overheating might require a cool-down period; an AV cable error would flag up all four red quadrants. The red-light combo I was getting reported was three red quadrants lit up. Three lights meant a 'general hardware' error, non-specific and factored around one or more issues.

Weeks passed, and the calls and console return rate escalated well above acceptable rates. Still, because of the non-specific nature of the errors, our engineers couldn't pinpoint the specific issue. All we knew was that heat retention and the internal effect of such was *something* to do with it.

Push came to shove, and a definitive crisis management response came.

In a meeting with Microsoft CEO Steve Ballmer, VP Marketing Peter Moore, and CXO Robbie Bach, proposed to take *all* affected consoles back with a first-class doorstep program to fix or replace customers' consoles within five days, not the standard 3-4 weeks it would typically take.

"This brand is dead if we don't do this," Peter stated as a fact to Ballmer. Steve Ballmer did the right thing to his credit and approved the cost on the spot.

The cost estimate was $1.15 billion, of which FedEx got $240 million. So impactful was this cost that it figured in the corporate Microsoft results reported to the markets as a $1 billion write-down.

The program included a three-year extended warranty, and together with the 5-day turnaround, the company embarked on a period that most of us would rather forget.

As Peter Moore intended, what became known as the Red Ring of Death (RRoD) was eventually handled in a first-class way. We did the right thing; we looked after our customers.

Silent hardware revisions started to address the issues, larger heatsinks, different circuit boards and component solder, all in a slightly aimless attempt at fixing the non-specific issues. Performance *did* improve through these revisions but never faded until the 'slim' version of the console came through, code name Trinity. The Xbox 360 S finally put the saga to bed once and for all.

Despite all the challenges, Xbox 360 was a success, practically matching PS3 hardware sales globally. It took Sony to have their worst PlayStation era and Xbox to have their best to get to these tied results, a result that just a few short years earlier had looked so unlikely.

But was it a tie? By the metric of hardware sales only, sure. Yes, Xbox 360 became the top-selling console in strongholds like the UK and Scandinavia around 2012, seven years after it first launched, but the best results were not published.

According to GfK, in 2012 in the UK, Xbox 360 had 46% of the total category spend. We were making more money than PS3 and Nintendo's Wii *combined*. By this metric, Xbox 360 punched above its weight and *won* this console generation.

Would history repeat itself and determine that Xbox would not win the forthcoming generation either?

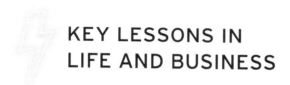

KEY LESSONS IN LIFE AND BUSINESS

SONY AND THE WHERE TO PLAY, HOW TO PLAY CHOICES

Sony put the Blu-Ray drive in the PS3, and other component factors meant the manufacturing cost of their PS3 console was disproportionately high.

This was a strategic choice to grow the install base of Blu-Ray. It worked but at a high cost.

Delays and the incremental costs passed on to the consumer put them at a disadvantage. We got a clear holiday season run in the market at a competitive price. Sony never recovered from a slow and expensive start.

CRISIS MANAGEMENT

The Red Ring of Death could've been the end of Xbox forever. But the executive team played the response to this perfectly and did the essential thing in crisis management:

They did the right thing.

Scott Galloway, founder of Section and professor at NYU

Stern School of Business, cites three key things in his brand management course you *must* do in a crisis:

1. Get a senior figurehead out in front of the issue in public.
2. Apologise promptly, own the issue.
3. Overcorrect in your response.

The response program was not a product recall but was not far off in terms of scale. Doorstep service and an extra warranty all contributed to shoring up the brand and ensuring all the work we'd done was not undone. Forever.

BY WHAT METRICS DO YOU MEASURE YOUR BUSINESS?

Xbox 360 won this generation, but not by the industry's metrics. Console sales in revenue and units were the benchmark for a long time, but Xbox showed the actual value of the ecosystem with a best-in-category revenue profile.

Isn't taking more share of wallet more important?

CHAPTER 22

VIDEO KILLED THE RADIO STAR

"**H**arv, the situation at work isn't good for anyone, is it?" my wife Natalie told me with her trademark honesty.

"We have a family now; you're exhausted from getting up at 5am to drive 120 miles a day to the office," she continued. "The office relocation is weighing on you and us. You're heading for a meltdown managing the long commute, your work and family life."

She was correct, as usual.

Since Xbox moved from London to Reading a few years earlier, my quick train ride was now a three-four hour round trip in the car. Despite some carpooling, after years of tolerating the drive, I felt like I couldn't do it any longer.

"I know, but the options are limited, aren't they?" I admitted.

"So, what're we going to do?" She pressed.

"We need a family meeting," I declared.

It was true that after 11 years at Xbox, I needed a new challenge. I wanted that challenge to be at Microsoft, but I set my parameters tightly, meaning I either tried to get a role at Microsoft back in London or I looked to Seattle and moved to HQ.

Natalie and I had been to Seattle recently; we'd looked around and discussed a move there. Getting a role in Xbox HQ wasn't the hurdle. The dichotomy was entirely personal.

By now, we had a little boy and proximity to family was an absolute priority, especially with both sets of our parents getting older. Despite my parents being unable to visit the US, I didn't mind travelling back, but Natalie isn't a lover of travel and starting a new life in the States, 4,781 miles from close family and friends, was more of a challenge for her.

After the meeting, we decided together that we wouldn't go to live in America. We'd lose more than we gained, so it was a personal decision.

At work, if Xbox 360 was the era that everything scaled and matured, it was also the era that everything got cyclical and predictable. This was good for the business but less so for me.

I was bored in my current role. So much so that I started a significant side project in the music business with Natalie and my sister-in-law that dominated all my free time for a couple of years. Although I didn't fully realise it at the time, I was subconsciously thinking about what was next in my life beyond what had become a very comfortable existence at Microsoft.

I was continuously looking to push myself. I needed more than Microsoft could provide in Europe.

A change in management had ushered in a new culture in the Xbox organisation. Robbie Bach, Chief Xbox Officer, elected to retire from Microsoft and was replaced by Don Mattrick, the former President of EA Studios.

The impact, from my perspective, was immediate. Ill-thought-out erratic requests and instructions started to come through. We had to do a Call of Duty custom-designed console in a third of the time it'd typically take. Not only was this a bad idea commercially, but our research and previous poor forecasts from the regions were also why we had never pursued one before, and the organisational impact was horrific. The Global and regional teams had to drop so much other work to get this through in the reduced time that doing a great job became just getting the job done. There *is* a difference.

This is what happens when, as I imagine it, two CEOs agree on a deal over brandy and hand it off to their respective teams. I knew I'd experience more of this CEO-knows-best approach in the coming years.

Regardless of the 'new noise' internally from a change in management, we were in top shape to start planning the forthcoming generation of Xbox. Codename, Durango, the Xbox One (yes, I know, it was the third iteration of Xbox).

The Global team were buttoned up, the collaboration fluid and the planning priorities and goals were laid out. Both Durango and 'Long Tail' (the gradual wind down and sunset of Xbox 360) were internal initiatives given equal priority and resourcing, a resultant lesson learnt from the crash landing of the original Xbox.

The clarity around preparation and planning for Durango and Long Tail was the best we'd experienced. This time, there were dedicated people who focused on the exit and entry plans for the generational changes.

Great go-to-market (GTM) assets, internal communication with accompanying roadshows, and cross-functional meetings brought a renewed sense of purpose and drive. Regarding preparation, neither the original Xbox nor the Xbox 360 had seen such alignment and clarity.

Aside from my day job of managing the hardware business, I put myself forward to lead in other areas of the Xbox business, and I made this clear in 1:1's with my manager, Jim.

"Jim, you know I need more of a challenge, whether in my current role or a new role within Microsoft," I said.

"I know, Harvey, I agree you need to be more challenged in this role after so long, but don't discount opportunities outside of Microsoft," he responded.

He got my attention; was he trying to offload me?

"Jim, I don't want to leave the Microsoft family, but eventually, I'll need to work back in London full-time."

"Consider all your options, Harvey. That's all I'm saying. Most importantly, know your value in the market. Whatever you decide to do, I'll support you."

Jim was a manager you wanted to work for, regardless of the logo above the door and one of only a few I've met in my whole career.

I started getting involved with projects on Xbox beyond my direct remit and loved the diversification. Something else that played to my strengths was the ability to adapt quickly.

One high-profile project was the retailer partner briefing for the new console generation. Hundreds of people across dozens and dozens of strategic retailers were invited to locations in the United Kingdom, France, and Germany, where we, together with colleagues from the Global team, would spend two whole days deep-diving into our next-generation plans.

So, everything was set, and we'd never been in such good shape, right? Wrong.

There were some grave concerns around positioning and some of the new features. The consensus was that the new TV component was interesting but not robust enough to worry existing TV providers. The proposition that you would 'have a relationship with your TV' was somewhat thin at best.

The internal belief at the highest level was that TV as a platform was ripe for reinvention and that the new Xbox would be the most significant change in how people consumed TV content for generations. To deliver that, you needed three key things:

1. The next-generation Kinect sensor (2.0) as your gesture-based input device.

2. The programming and content needed to be best in class at a local country level.
3. The user experience needed to be seamless and effortless.

The new Kinect was a huge technological step, and everything the first version *should've* been. However, to facilitate delivering the TV proposition to everyone, everyone had to have a Kinect, which became a mandatory requirement, not an optional one.

To make it mandatory, Xbox only offered the Xbox One with a Kinect. You couldn't buy an Xbox One without Kinect (2.0), which drove an extra $100 onto the cost of the Xbox. If you weren't interested in TV or Kinect, you had to buy it anyway.

The country-level content plan for TV was lacking. Only three out of the twenty-seven countries in my EMEA region would have local TV content available at launch. It'd take months and months for all the other countries to get the TV content that was local to them. Thus, in twenty-four countries in my region, the TV proposition was only considered for the USA, UK, France, and Germany. There was nothing in it for them.

To enable TV as an experience, you could get an over-the-air Xbox TV adapter at an additional cost. Or plug your existing set-top box into the Xbox One and control the whole lot via the Xbox. But only the most basic functionalities from the set-top box could be controlled via the Xbox, even if the content could be displayed. If you wanted to record a programme, you had to reach for the original remote from your cable TV provider.

The focus on TV was a big concern internally, especially as it felt very selective at a country level. We all understood the challenges in making such an endeavour happen. Our problems were waylaid because all internal prioritisation was around the core gamer and having a great lineup of games.

We were blessed with a perfect launch portfolio. Key racing, football and action games, all top franchises from day one, were available for the Xbox One. The first priority was to 'secure the core early' so, in this context, everything else was secondary for the launch window.

The TV proposition could 'catch up' once we'd secured the core gamer community.

Another big challenge, and the biggest one, was the new digital rights management (DRM) systems on the console.

Historically, games sold on optical media (discs) would be traded second-hand at retailers for credit or cash to underwrite the cost of the next purchase for a core gamer. Considering that in 2012/2013, a core gamer would play a new game every six weeks, you can appreciate that it was an expensive hobby at $60 per game.

The secondary games market enabled gamers to buy and trade in to facilitate playing as many games as possible.

Critically, it also enabled retailers to profit more from reselling the same game. Many retailers made way more profit from the secondary market than in other areas of their business. According to analysis done by Joost van Dreunen in his book 'One Up', Gamestop would net $162 from the lifetime sales of re-selling a $60 title over and over again by way of trade-ins. The original publisher would make $24 from a one-time sale as they didn't share in the revenue once a game had been sold more than once.

Yet the Publishers and creators took most of the financial risk in making and bringing a game to market.

Xbox One's DRM meant that your licence for the game was on the disc and, in effect, would be locked to that console. You couldn't resell it, nor was it easy to take your game disc to your friend's house to play as it was locked to your console back home.

It might've technically killed the secondary market for retailers, but it also killed how our core audience shared their experiences with their friends. It killed the fun, too.

These details, known internally to be very contentious for our partners, were *deliberately* not shared at the pre-release retail briefings. We knew that it would've created so much flux for the launch that it was held back for an announcement at another time.

You'd have a case to say it was less than transparent.

Unsurprisingly, during town hall meetings and feedback loops through the correct channels, the two main themes of concern were DRM and the very broad positioning as 'the all-in-one entertainment system.'

We had a sense at the time that feedback, born out of data, was falling on deaf ears at the highest level.

I sat in one Global Town Hall meeting where the questions and feedback were responded to badly. The answers seemed to have very little to do with the questions.

"The data shows that it's games, games, games that our audience cares about. Only 1% of Xbox owners use an Xbox primarily as a multimedia box," stated the staffer. "Why are we chasing the multi-media position so prominently when no one cares?"

It was an undeniable truth.

The response was an academic, aspirational rallying call to 'own the living room.' Nothing specific and certainly no direct answers to the questions. It was like the management throwing flak up to distract us from reality so they could chase their visions.

The visions went beyond just TV, however. Convergence and broader-based services were also a key theme, even in the Xbox 360 'long tail'.

Xbox Fitness (powered by Kinect) was a total wipe-out. A half-arsed attempt at being Peleton before Peleton came to be, it was a proposition aimed at an audience who cared little about fitness. Even for those who did, only having an English-language option with California-based 'hard-bods' was a cultural mismatch in markets outside the USA.

Xbox Music might have shown greater promise, given it was to be hard installed on Windows 8 PCs on the main dashboard. I was drafted in by the Senior Leadership Team (SLT) in EMEA to give my experienced view on the endeavour and how we should consider strategic investments into music.

"Only Spotify is the main *significant* competitor, but they were so far ahead of the rest of the pack, and our Xbox Music offering would need major strategic investment," I stated in the boardroom as I ran the SLT through the numbers.

"Investment would need to be the offering itself and the human capital required to make it a success," I continued. "Our catalogue with record labels is half of what Spotify has."

Availability was initially on Windows 8 PC desktop and Windows Phone, and when the Android and iOS versions would come, they were impoverished experiences in comparison. Despite wanting to, I had a complimentary employee subscription, and I still couldn't live with it.

My advice to the SLT in my leadership presentation was as follows...

"We need to significantly invest in these various areas [points to details on the slides] to get to 'table stakes' with Spotify even to be considered in this market," I concluded.

The leadership in EMEA swallowed deep, and you could feel the oxygen level thinning as the penny dropped.

Consequently, Xbox Music in EMEA largely got ignored and bumped along for a couple of years until it morphed into Microsoft Groove. Then, Microsoft inevitably put the category out to pasture and transferred all remaining Groove subscribers to Spotify. Oh, the irony!

I won't even waste your time by writing about the Xbox Fitness Band [think Fitbit]. I successfully got that killed off in

Europe (with market data) before it physically existed. Imagine my reaction when the same internal protagonists launched the Microsoft Fitness Band a couple of years later.

Yup, you guessed it. Two years later, it got pulled from marketing and written off as a bad idea.

Despite efforts to broaden and converge with Microsoft Windows, not all efforts were in vain. The 'Metro' design style that was the visual cornerstone of Windows 8 also got rolled out across the Xbox and Phone interfaces for the first time, giving Microsoft a unified platform look and feel for the first time.

Long tail and Durango planning aside, the main event of what would become known as the Xbox One would be the public announcements.

At the Electronic Entertainment Expo (E3) in LA, Xbox was to reveal all the details about the Xbox One and give live demos to a global audience of retailers, journalists, and core gamers worldwide watching the live video stream.

It's fair to say that E3 announcements, especially for a new console generation, are a huge deal. They happen only once every five-seven years as a new generation of machines prepares to come to market and are live-streamed around the world.

We never had the strong sense that the world was waiting for the next Xbox. As the challenger brand, we'd always had to punch above our weight and work twice as hard to get half the distance. This was different, though...our phone constantly rang, and there were slews of enquiries and partnership interest from companies that would previously have dismissed us.

And we were ready. All our ducks were in a row. We were confident, especially in the launch line up and future roadmap.

What could possibly go wrong?

The messaging, that's what. How Xbox got its messaging *so wrong* at a *critical* time in front of *the* biggest and most attentive audience is still an industry mystery.

Growing up, I remember a friend's father shouting at the TV, hitting or kicking it if something went technically wrong with it or some 'celebrity' said something he'd taken exception to. Something might get thrown across the room in the TV's general direction.

I never thought I'd evoke those memories again, let alone replicate them in the office! We all sat around in the recreation area of the Xbox office on the sofas, tuned into the live stream from Los Angeles.

Our expectations were *so* high that our confidence was robust. The wind was in our sails.

And within a few very short minutes came the content announcements. 'Ah', I thought, 'our Stella launch lineup is going to shine now.' Only, what *I* saw and heard was...

"TV, TV, TV, TV... " said the Xbox executives.

"You're going to have a relationship with your TV," they added.

"Xbox will be the new water cooler moment in the office. We're announcing the new Halo."

"Ah," I thought, "A stellar game at last.'

"Announcing Halo, the movie!" they finished.

What the... argh!

What happened to the games? I counted nearly 60 references to TV in the announcement. I counted endless generic references to 'sports', and the only game that seemed to get any meaningful airtime was Call of Duty. A top game, but the focus was the rendering quality of a character in the game. To make matters worse, the character was a dog.

You couldn't make it up.

So, there you have it, we announced TV, sports, and a dog. What happened to our planning? Our objective of 'secure the core' first? The company had clearly forgotten the first rule of marketing; you're *not* the customer.

By focusing on what the executives aspired to [TV], they forgot that the core audience for Xbox is hardcore gamers that care very little about that stuff. You'll recall I can even put a number on it. In my role at Xbox, I knew from data that less than 1% of owners bought an Xbox primarily for its broad media capability. A clearer and harder fact you won't find.

But we had to add *more* self-inflicted injury.

The DRM announcement of the Xbox One plus the fact that including the Kinect sensor to the package as a mandatory requirement, adding $100 to the overall cost, were (as we predicted) massively unpopular. Just about as popular as a pork chop at a bar mitzvah!

When it was all said and done an hour later, and there was nothing left in the office to throw at the TV, we sat silently, just looking at each other. We were empty shells; our own people had hollowed us out. What had the execs done? Could they have listened to the feedback less? Could they have read the market worse?

But worse was to come! Because Sony would be announcing their PlayStation 4 just 24 hours later. How would they respond? Very well, that's how.

We watched the Sony press conference the next day, and they'd clearly been adjusting their plans based on the 'gift' we'd given them:

- First announcement: a slew of quality games
- Second announcement: no DRM and support for the secondary games market
- Third announcement: $100 cheaper than Xbox. And an open and declared love for gamers around the world

They played to their core audience and simultaneously kicked Xbox in the nuts. Hard.

And it fucking hurt. It hurt so bad because it was all *so*

avoidable. The company execs made choices that contradicted the clear objectives in planning by focusing on what the company aspired to on paper. It wanted to win the living room by 'reinventing TV' but at the expense of the customers who'd made Xbox what it was.

Within 24 hours, our confidence was bust. The wind was very much in Sony's sails.

What happened next was no surprise. After Sony's press conference, negative feedback from the market started to come in like a handwritten note wrapped around a brick, thrown in our general direction. Within days, battered by the feedback, the top management sent a communication to the whole Xbox team worldwide.

"We've listened."

"We've taken the feedback onboard."

"We'll make big changes, but our launch time frame doesn't change."

They listened to the market because it told them it was a dud, and the consequence was that PlayStation would get all the backing. Why didn't they listen to their own people? Or read the market? After all, we'd had the foresight to read it.

So, what of the changes?

- First, the DRM system that locked games to a player's console would be dropped.
- Second. We'd focus on games more.
- Third. We'd keep Kinect in the box with the high price tag (sigh).

That first part was the kicker. To drop DRM, the code for the *entire* operating system would need a massive rewrite. In short, it felt like we were starting over.

But such work takes years... we were launching in just six months!

The company asked the developers to work nights and weekends. More developers were brought in, their families would be bused to 'visit Daddy or Mummy'. It was a genuine around-the-clock operation with an outcome that was far from guaranteed.

I had to redo the launch planning. Every console launch is fraught with uncertainty. The ramp-up to consistent manufacturing yields for new technology is a tightrope for all concerned at the best of times.

But under these circumstances, we all felt way more heat than usual. To make the dates, the Xbox One would ship *without* an operating system. It'd be a useless box of components until you plugged it into the internet via a cable to download the software to make it work.

This allowed the developers many more weeks to work on the code whilst we were able to ship the physical boxes. It was the only possible chance we had to meet the launch as if nothing was wrong.

And somehow, we made the date.

One month before launch, I emailed our team to confirm that our allocated units weren't just 'on the water' (shipping from China) but had arrived in regional distribution and were being prepared to be shipped to meet our prior commitments with our retail partners.

250,000 Xbox One consoles were shipped to plan for the European launch day. The sacrifice and dedication of the developers made it happen.

The impact on the internal teams was massive but not as huge as the longer-term impact of the wrong positioning and messaging.

It was no real surprise that soon after the first few weeks of sales were in, they disappointed. Don Mattrick quickly moved on from Microsoft. With Xbox under new management again and a console generation lost before it started, it was time to move on to new pastures for me too.

But where?

KEY LESSONS IN LIFE AND BUSINESS

YOU AREN'T THE CUSTOMER

The Microsoft executives all failed to read the market and the research properly. They also failed to listen to the internal teams who knew the market and our target audience better than they did.

To make matters far worse, in my opinion, they considered they knew better and went chasing a dream of owning the living room. This mantra has deep roots in the organisation as it was the fear of Sony's more general dominance of the living room with TV, DVD, movies and the like that got the original Xbox green-lit as a project.

Top management at Xbox had no humility at this time until retailer feedback stopped them in their tracks.

It was one of the worst cases of self-inflicted harm you'll see in business. And one that was so unnecessary.

KEEP THE PROPER FOCUS AND GO ALL IN

Fitness, music and gadgets were all a failure for Xbox. Not because they were all without merit, but in many cases, they were half-arse attempts passed off as a big commitment.

Music could have worked, but the desire to invest heavily in a combative market was a huge barrier. The lack of investment in Europe in music made doubling down on our focus on our games business even more straightforward.

KNOW YOUR VALUE

I was ready to make a change, but I'd initially set my move criteria too tightly – move to Seattle or a different Microsoft team in London, but neither happened by design or default.

Candid discussions with my manager helped me realise my value to an organisation and open my mind to other possibilities. It was only then that my long-held suspicion that I'd outgrown my role at a company that I loved became an undeniable fact.

The outcome was the hardest decision I have ever had to make.

▲ London, 2002. My first official corporate head shots were for Xbox.

▶ Athens, Greece. I addressed the Greek media at an Xbox trade event. This really confirmed I'd swapped guitars and cables for PowerPoint and a talk track!

▲ Let battle commence! I got caught in the middle of the HD video format war between Sony and Toshiba. Most of us knew how it would end before it started.

▼ The Greatest! I attended the Xbox media conference in Los Angeles, May 10th, 2004, with Muhammad Ali, Robbie Bach (left), and Marshall Faulk. Bach was later replaced by Don Mattrick (right) as head of Xbox.

Photo credit: Bloomberg

EPILOGUE

The story you have just read started in the early 1980s and concluded in 2013. Only, it doesn't end here, as I'm still living it, and the next decade(s) will be the basis of the next book.

Life has a strange way of calibrating outcomes. Sheer luck and serendipity play a massive part, and the notion of someone's personal life being utterly separate from their professional life is false.

The definition of luck is the success or failure apparently brought by chance rather than through one's own actions. However, looking back on my story, I'd like to think that my actions created my luck.

As I sit here in 2024, let's take the opportunity to catch up with some of the key characters you've just read about...

AC/DC

The album that started it all off for me in 1980, *Back in Black*, became the second highest-selling album of all time, moving 50 million copies. Only Michael Jackson's *Thriller* did better (70 million).

The band kept their main line-up together for decades except for having revolving drummers to replace original drummer Phil Rudd who suffered from issues ranging from substance abuse to legal challenges.

Tragically, death is not a new concept to the band. In early 1980, their lead singer Bon Scott died in London due to acute alcohol poisoning, with the coroner's official report concluding that Scott had died of "death by misadventure."

But another hammer blow was to hit the band years later. Original band member Malcolm Young had to retire from the band in 2014 due to ill health and was replaced by his nephew, Stevie Young.

It was later reported that Malcolm had been diagnosed with dementia and admitted to a nursing home where he could receive full-time care. Three years later, Malcolm died at the age of just 64.

Malcolm was the engine room, the driving force and the band's unofficial leader.

Incredibly, the band are still together, despite other significant challenges like singer Brian Johnson losing his hearing. Yet, demand for their music has never been greater.

The first week of sales in the UK for their last album, *Power Up* in 2020, was the fastest in the market at the time and went to number one on the charts around the world, including in the United States.

The world still cannot get enough of this band. Even after nearly 50 years!

AC/DC are why I got into music and the *business* of music. Without them, this book and my career, as I know it, wouldn't exist. I was always touched by how grounded they were when I met them, and by Malcolm's thoughtfulness when he sent me a thank you note, alongside a signed copy of what would become the *Bonfire* box set that I helped them with.

HERMAN'S HERMITS

My boss (and friend), Derek 'Lek' Leckenby, died in 1994, but the band continued with just one original member, Barry 'Bean' Whitwam.

The band's line-up is a merry-go-round of other members, but that's of no natural consequence. What is of significance is the legality of the name and its ownership. As documented, Bean's band can no longer tour in America, something I was privileged to be able to do with them years earlier. Peter Noone's version of the band has the rights to the lucrative US market.

Incredibly, the band is *still* going strong and touring into their 60th year.

SMALLTOWN HEROES

If there was ever a band that had it all going for them, it was Smalltown Heroes, but without massive financial investment, and I mean *massive*, the writing was on the wall.

The band defied the odds with two albums recorded for Global/BMG (one of which was released in the UK and German markets) and countless tours and champions collected along the way. But, without that helpful tool called the internet, it still wasn't enough to find an audience large enough to commercialise where the return on the investment would've made sense.

Baz, Chris, Tony and Kev, unfortunately, became part of the enormous failure rate that plagues musicians.

The lads are still in music to this day. Kev and Tony play on the local circuit in various bands; Chris lives in New Zealand and, for many years, built an audio branding business, but the story of note is what happened to Baz.

In the biggest twist of fate, irony and serendipity, Baz is now the frontman for The Stranglers. Yes, THE Stranglers.

The band he followed as a teenage fan, the band the Smalltown Heroes toured with in Europe. Twice! Baz ended up in the band and has been their frontman for over twenty years.

The Stranglers will tour for their 50th anniversary in 2024, and I, for one, will be down the front (and backstage) celebrating.

Those who know Baz will know that for decades of struggle, no one could deny his 'overnight success.'

SAM ALDER AND EG MUSIC

When I left EG, my final salary cheque bounced, although it was made good a few weeks later. But without Sam Alder replying to my speculative fax, future careers would never have happened, my own included.

For this, it's with the utmost gratitude that I respect Sam and the team who supported us. Despite all the odds, he took me on and gave the band a shot. Sam invested his own money, but it turned out that it was money he possibly could ill afford.

No one knew the whole financial picture until the 27th of April 2018, when Sam was declared bankrupt in court, owing Lloyds Bank International £2.6m with the backdrop that he had an existing negative asset position of over £6 million.

In passing judgement, His Worship the High Bailiff, John Needham, noted, "I found that the Defendant's well-mannered exterior was accompanied by a steely determination, shown by the degree to which the Defendant has fought this case up to this point, to make things difficult for the Claimant. I am of the view that every move the Defendant has made in these proceedings has been carefully measured by him. The timings of applications, the making of last-minute offers, the lack of early disclosure, the lack of payment of anything and the admission of last-minute evidence only when the alternative was likely to be an immediate order in bankruptcy, portray a person who is not as straightforward as one could hope for."

The future of EG was on life support soon after I left, but they hobbled on officially for years, I suspect living off small royalty cheques from Killing Joke's publishing business. The London office in Chelsea was gone; all but one staff member was gone, and the registered office became a home address.

According to official filings at Companies House, EG Music Limited was dissolved on 2nd July 2019.

Sam had to resign from his own company, the official **Termination of appointment** of Samuel George Alder as a director on 27th April 2018 was his bankruptcy date.

This is no coincidence. In the UK, you're not allowed to be a company director once you're bankrupt.

One final **Unaudited abridged account** was filed, made up to the 31st of December 2018; then, it was curtains for EG.

This was a show that would *not* go on.

STEVE BUSH AND MARSHALL BIRD

When Stereophonics got signed to Richard Branson's new label V2, after the Smalltown Heroes showcase, it gave Steve Bush and Marshall Bird the break they needed. They went on to produce five million of the nine million UK album sales (55%) across the band's first three and ultimately most commercially successful albums.

Not half bad, given the *first* album they produced was *Human Soup* by Smalltown Heroes…

None of us could've foreseen that Stereophonics would be awarded six multi-platinum album certifications, one platinum and six gold; one of their singles has been awarded a multi-platinum certification, three platinum, one gold and nine silver (source: BPI). They have sold over 9,000,000 albums in the UK and 5,400,000 singles.

Not half bad for the Smalltown Heroes support band!

Steve and Marsh were very much part of our gang; they had the talent and put the hard work in. Steve and I were flatmates for a couple of years, and I can personally attest that he gave everything to make things happen. No one outside the band and yours truly put more human effort into it than he did.

Bushy, I tip my hat to ya.

VIRGIN/INTERPLAY

I loved working at Virgin and, latterly, the US arm, Interplay. The irreverence, the independent spirit, the people and some great products made for an intoxicating mix of work hard, play harder.

Chaos internally was rife, as communications to staff were non-existent, and what we did know turned out to be a farce. It created an inertia for the company where nothing could be achieved. It didn't take long for the newly owned Virgin-Interplay to haemorrhage people.

Matt returned to the United States and headed up development for a US gaming start-up, which ironically, years later, was acquired by Microsoft.

I started my adventure at Microsoft, as the presence in the office got hollowed out person by person.

In June 2004, the new owners, Titus, declared themselves bankrupt. In January 2005, a French district commercial court declared Titus bankrupt with a €33 million (US$43.8 million) debt.

It was game over.

XBOX

From just 12 staff when I joined to nearly 80 when I left, the Xbox went on to become part of the social fabric of the living room, tapping into and, in many cases, leading gaming culture.

The growing pains of the first Xbox were understandable, given the urgency and context in which it was launched.

The Xbox 360 was the next generation's hero, where good key bets, the value proposition, and organisational alignment all played a part in its success.

The missed opportunity of the Xbox One (the third Xbox.... grrr) resulted in years in the wilderness but years that new management made the most of. Getting their shit together, testing new ideas in the market, and getting ready for the next and fourth Xbox.

The Xbox Series X|S is a triumph of technology, market orientation and humility to learn from mistakes. Many things in X|S were 'in the hopper' in the previous generation, and I credit the team for pulling it out of the bag, especially the Global Head of Xbox, Phil Spencer.

It's been a long time since we played five-a-side football together in Reading, UK, when Phil was General Manager, EMEA Microsoft Game Studios.

FAITH AND BEING A MINORITY

This is a theme that I touched on briefly in the first chapter but didn't think about until the latter stages of editing.

Why did I only include this late on in the process? Well, frankly, I was scared to death to talk about it, but my editor and some of the advanced readers of the manuscript picked up on it. I found some much-needed bravery.

So, here it is. I am a reasonably observant, practising Jew, but I wasn't always.

The antisemitic bullying I received at school definitely affected key choices I've made in my life. It influenced me to send my kids to a faith school, so they didn't suffer as I did. Even my wife, Natalie, was slightly surprised at how strong my feelings about schooling were.

She went to a Jewish secondary school. I didn't.

Despite being seemingly ambivalent about my faith for *many* years, I actively chose to marry within the faith and have a religious wedding. Until I met Natalie, I wasn't that observant, but I had made a personal decision to 'marry in' or not at all.

'Marrying in' meant I had to be <u>all in</u>.

Regardless, even to this day, I've always been very sensitive, telling anyone I work with that I'm Jewish. Out of fear. Fear that they'll judge me, not like me, or persecute me somehow. Only when I know someone well enough will I tell them. Even then, most people's perception or understanding of someone Jewish is sometimes laughable. I *still* get questions like...

"When did you move to England?" [I was born here].

"What was it like growing up in Jerusalem?!" [I have no idea; I grew up in Manchester].

"Wow, you speak English really well" [I *am* English].

"You don't look Jewish..." [WTF do 'we' look like?].

It goes to the heart of the matter. People know nothing. It's not laughable at all. Antisemitism is on the rise; in the past two years, officially recorded antisemitic incidents in the UK have doubled.

And if my kids want to go to university, we're going to have 'the talk'. UK universities have been officially found to be unwelcoming and hostile places for Jewish students.

The more things change, the more they (sadly) stay the same.

ME

And so, to yours truly. Well, you might've heard I wrote a book?!

Jokes aside, it's been one hell of a ride, and the ride will continue in the next book, covering my time at other corporations in other categories and the challenges and opportunities this has brought.

After working for 40 years, I still have something in the tank, but my current life as a consultant, mentor, teacher and now author was always my destiny. However, I can only say that with the benefit of hindsight, the 20-year-old me would've had no idea this would've been my destination.

The path of a career isn't linear; it's a marathon, not a sprint, and outcomes are far from guaranteed. Yet, it's the journey, not the destination you'll live in daily; make sure you embrace it.

Some say that the past is an indicator of the future. Yet, we live in the present, and your future has not yet been written.

Only you can write it.

Thank you so much for reading my story. I look forward to reading yours.

ACKNOWLEDGMENTS

FAMILY

Natalie Lee, who encouraged me when I doubted,
reminded me when I paused and tells me how it is.

Zack and Joshua, who one day will read this
and realise Daddy was far naughtier than they
ever were and that nothing is impossible.

Dad, Debra and the whole Lee family.
Now you know what you never knew.

The London chapter; Hannah, Kelly, and
Daniella Erez. Moshe, rest in peace, boss.

INDELIBLE CONNECTIONS

Distance and time apart mean nothing to dear old friends.

Baz Warne, Chris Warne, Tony Roffe, Kevin
Scott, Leonie Leckenby, Peter Knight Jr., Chris
East, Jeff Singer, Steve Robinson, David Lawrence,
David Kaitiff. Derek Leckenby (RIP).

MORE THAN COLLEAGUES

There are simply too many to mention. You are all part
of my life and, by definition, this book, but to those
who had a direct and lasting impact...thank you.

Ilia Kuznetsov, Andrei Mochola, Steve Bush,
Marshall Bird, Matt Findley,
Richard King, Jeroen van Beem.

THE BACKSTAGE PASS TEAM

I could not have produced this book without the following
amazing human beings:

Sarah Oliver – Editor
Lawrence Chapman – Proofing and copy
Rachael O'Flaherty – Proofing
Faye Lloyd – Cover design
Julie Karen Hodgins – Interior design and layout
Henry Willard – Sound editor (audiobook)
Meryl Evans – Legal

Special thanks to my advanced reading team, who dedicated
their time and energy to the cause.

Justin Vaughan-Brown   Amit Alagh
Lauren Kennedy   Renae Bradley-McBride
Gabrielle Tenaglia   Simon Moran
Steven Sutherland

PATRONS

My sincere and humble thanks go to the individuals and companies who showed their support early on.

Simon Hayhurst

Div Manickam

Heather Quist

Jason Chien

Stanley Harris OBE

Andrei Mochola

Linda Franklin

Vanessa Hoermann
von Hoerbach

Jeroen van Beem

Jonny Mosesson

Ilya Kuznetsov

Riccardo de Rinaldini

David Lawrence

Jeff Singer

Michael Lee

Jonathan Elford

Dennis Xie

Julien Sauvage

Irit Schwartz

Rinel Levitin

Veronica Carlson

Paul Fox

Lee Dunn

Michelle Picoto

Maria Luisa Liuzzo

Ruheene Masand Jaura

Sara Jacobs

Sam Filer

Scott Huson

Zoe Yates

Charlotte Hershman

Ricky Singh

Matt Marchington

Mark Hilditch
from Hilditch Guitars

Chris Bain
from Player One Consulting

Rohit Jain

Belinda Goodall

Renat Gersch

Jack Farrow

Stefan Kremel

Kristin Miltner-Zubrzycki

Jessica Hall

Steve Robinson

Ivan Buric

Keenan Cronyn

Peter Harrison

Sean Broderick

Deborah Dalgleish

Rosemary Clancy

Gab Bujold

Billy Tucker

Lodi Elaridi

Rich and Josie King
from Product Marketing Alliance

Thomas Madden

Stevie Langford

Royce Allen Quizora

Pedro Yiakoumi

Nasi Rwigema

Mark Lacey

Jon Sayer

Georgia Horsley

Beth Walker

Amelia Wilson

Zoe Koumbouzi

Peter Kortvel

Emma Stratton
from Punchy.co

Tamara Grominsky
from PMM Camp

Ian Hameroff
from Fulcrum Group

Marija Perinić
from Word Nerd

Jason Oakley
from Productive PMM

Vivian Liu

Milton Keynes UK
Ingram Content Group UK Ltd.
UKHW010057060224
437294UK00008B/432